Wood for Sheep

The Unauthorized Settlers Cookbook

Chris-Rachael Oseland

First Edition

Acknowledgements and Thanks

This book would not be possible without the wonder that is the Settlers of Catan board game franchise. If you don't own a copy of Settlers of Catan, you are missing out on life. Seriously. Put this book down immediately and go to your nearest game shop, Amazon, or the Mayfair Games website. Play a few times and you'll understand how a board game can inspire a cookbook.

Thank you to Klaus Teuber for bringing Settlers of Catan into the world back in 1995. Settlers ushered in a board game renaissance here in the United States and continues to be the most popular gateway game for introducing people to a whole new world of fun. I've made so many great friends through gaming.

Speaking of friends I met through gaming, thank you to Samantha Reisz for many nights of helping me flesh out the concept for this book and afternoons keeping me company while photographing that night's epic gamer dinner. This book wouldn't be nearly as nerdy without you.

Table of Contents

INTRODUCTION: REAL GAMERS DON'T ORDER PIZZA

Put down your pitchforks.

That sad truth was the original inspiration for this book. Whenever I game, two things invariably happen. First, a generous gamer who has somehow miraculously reached adulthood without any food allergies or dietary restrictions will offer to buy everyone pizza. Yay! Second, half the people in the room say, man, they wish they could eat pizza, but one has Celiac disease and another is lactose intolerant. For them, pizza might as well be poison. Then at least one other person quietly coughs that they're either a vegetarian or a paleo/primal dieter. By the time everyone with limited diet has bowed out, you realize the person who suggested pizza is the only person in the room who can safely eat it.

I hate situations like that. Too often, the poor, generous gamer who just wanted to top off everyone's fuel tanks so the group could keep playing without interruption now feels like a jerk. That's not right. Feeding a mixed group of geeks is hard.

This ongoing problem left me seriously pondering the best way to feed a big group of geeks. The most efficient answer was to tell them all to brown bag it since keeping up with everyone's specialized dietary needs can be a full time job. That isn't a very satisfying answer, though. Food isn't just a set of mandatory building blocks for cellular construction and repair. Eating together is social, and it should be fun.

Even if you don't play the game this book is based on, you recognize those red, green, and yellow hexes as an iconic part of geek culture. Lay out a hex shaped spread in those colors and you're automatically flying your geek flag. Plus, the edible hex maps look amazing. Each one is tailored to fit multiple dietary restrictions. As an extra bonus, most of them honestly aren't that hard to prepare.

I hope this book is helpful for any geeks struggling to figure out how to feed a group of people whose digestive systems all seem to be at war. I promise, no matter how physically limited or just plain picky they are, it really is possible to invite almost all of your friends over for the same meal. Pick up some cheap, disposable hex shaped dishes and you can even do it with style.

WHERE DO I GET THOSE AWESOME HEX SHAPED DISHES?

All the plastic dishes you see in this cookbook are actually hexagonal weigh boats manufactured by Scientific Equipment of Houston. I bought mine on Amazon.com. At press time for this book, you can get 100 of the medium sized (two cup) weigh boats for around $20, including shipping. One hundred of the small (1/2 cup) ones will run you closer to $15. You need 19 hexes to make a board, so each batch gets you enough supplies for five boards, plus a couple spare dishes.

The hexes are designed to be lightweight and disposable. Treat them the same way you treat disposable plastic plates from the grocery store.

You can find similar, inexpensive hex shaped disposable dishes manufactured by Small Wonders or Universal Medical. I'm not getting a kickback from any of these companies. I just want you to be able to find affordable hex shaped dishes, because those really complete the look.

Before starting this book, I did look into reusable hexagon shaped serveware. The dishes I found cost anywhere from $40-$180 each. For the cost of 19 dishes, you could afford the gorgeous Settlers of Catan 3D Collector's Edition (which is a better investment.) I want to keep all of this affordable and fun for your average gamer, so really, go get the disposable hexagon shaped weigh boats of your choice.

If, for whatever reason, you don't want to pick up some disposable plastic hexes, you can achieve 80% of the effect for most boards with hex shaped cookie cutters, a 15" or larger pizza baking sheet, and a lot of patience. Start with the center hex. Carefully stuff your food into the cookie cutter, let it rest for at least 30 seconds, then gently lift the cookie cutter. Put it down next to one of your food hex's six sides and repeat the process.

It's unsatisfying and nerve wracking, but you can actually make most of these boards with a single hex cookie cutter. That will run you about $6 instead of $15-20. Only you can decide if it's really worth the hassle. Wait. That's not true. I've done it both ways so you don't have to, and I can say with authority that the $9 savings isn't worth the Hulk-like rage you'll feel if you waste your time with just a cookie cutter.

WHAT OTHER SUPPLIES DO I NEED?

I tried to make this cookbook as accessible as possible. You really only need two special items - the hexagonal weigh boats and some hexagonal cookie cutters. I picked up a hexagon cookie cutter set with six graduated sizes for about $15, but you can get a single hex cookie cutter the same size as the hex dishes for about $6. You can find an assortment of sizes, prices, and collections at local craft stores, restaurant supply stores, Amazon.com or Etsy.com. The good folks at Mayfair Games also sell an official Settlers of Catan cookie cutter in the exact size of a Settlers of Catan tile. You can show them some support and get the perfect sized hex by buying directly through Mayfair Games.

SIZE MATTERS

The ½ cup small hex dishes require nine cups of food to fill. That's more than you think. The larger medium hex dishes fit two cups of food each. That's 38 cups of food. To put that in perspective, that's enough to fill four gallon sized milk jugs. If you're having four or five people over to have dinner and play a board game, you will have food leftover. Plan in advance and either have plenty of containers for leftovers or send everyone home with food for tomorrow's lunch.

SETTING UP THE BOARDS

If you take a good look at the green beans and asparagus (my two favorite forests) you'll notice they're mostly undressed. You'll also notice they stand up proud and strong like the fake trees they represent. These two things are related. You can make some very attractive tree shapes with fresh, dry vegetables, but once they're lubed up with tasty olive oil, butter, or spices, they become the world's most frustrating mess. Take my word on it when I say more often than not, you want to present the cooked asparagus and green beans unseasoned. Leave a subtle little bowl of dressing off to one side. Once everyone destroys your hard work by serving themselves, they can also douse the veggies in sauce.

DEFINING THE TERRITORIES

For the themed maps, I tried to stick with the color scheme of red hills, green forests, yellow fields, dark mountains, a white desert, and yellow/green pasture.

For the building cost inspired recipes, I had to decide how I wanted to define bricks, wood, sheep, ore, and grain.

Two of those are obvious. Sheep give you either lamb meat or sheep's milk. Grain can mean pretty much any edible grass (wheat, oats, barley, rice, etc.)

Wood was a little trickier, and bricks just turned into any edible building block the right shade of red. You'll see plenty of tomatoes and red bell peppers.

But what can you do with ore? Humans will eat darn near anything that isn't a rock, and if the rock is salt, we'll make an exception. I freely admit I took some liberties. Hopefully, you'll find them worth the flavor.

DIETARY RESTRICTIONS

As a second generation geek, I know if you get five of us together, three will have some kind of serious food restriction. I've done my best to make this book as inclusive as possible.

While you can frequently add bacon to gain a victory point, I chose not to use pork or shellfish in any of the core recipes for the sake of our Kosher, Halal and nitrate allergic friends.

The Nicoise Salad, Breakfast Taco, Nacho, Roasted Root Vegetable and Home Made Dips boards were designed with gamers in mind who have celiac disease, wheat allergies, or who are just avoiding wheat due to assorted low carb diets. The Southern, Paella, Indian, Middle Eastern, and Cold Summer Salad boards are also easy to modify to make them wheat free.

Vegans can enjoy the Cold Summer Salad, Root Vegetable, and Paella boards while octo-lavo (dairy and egg eating) vegetarians can enjoy all of those plus the boards for Quick Breads, Biscuit, Waffle, and Home Made Dips.

Gamers keeping a primal or paleo diet can turn the breakfast taco board into a morning scramble or enjoy the less board shaped items from the Building Cost recipes such as the rosemary stalk grilled cherry tomatoes with lamb kabobs.

If you've won the diverse geek lottery and need something to feed a mixed group with Kosher, Halal, celiac, vegetarian, and primal players, I recommend starting with the Salad Nicoise. Tuna is considered parve (neither meat nor dairy) in Kosher and doesn't have specific butchering guidelines in Halal, so those players can eat everything on the board. You don't have any grains, so the people with gluten sensitivities or who are restricting wheat are covered. The primal players will stay away from the potatoes, but everything else is fair game. Likewise, the vegetarians won't eat the tuna, but that's in self contained dishes where the meat doesn't touch anything else. Everyone should be able to eat at least 5 out of 6 things on the board.

Now that you have everyone covered, each player can easily assemble their own specialized salad while all sharing the same meal together. It's like magic.

In fact, due to the modular nature of these boards, no two foods touch at all. The boards look great for gaming purposes while incidentally making it a lot easier for people with different diets to eat together. This strict hex segregation is also great when feeding plain old picky eaters or anyone who gets uncomfortable when their foods touch. I hope you can use the core principles behind these boards to assemble meals all your friends can eat together.

To make things easier, I've provided a detailed appendix divided up by specific dietary needs. I didn't include Kosher or Halal in the appendix because that's nearly the entire book. You won't find any pork or shellfish recipes. However, there are a few recipes that aren't Kosher because meat and dairy are used in the same meal. When in doubt, ask your Jewish friends for guidance or stick with the entirely vegetarian options.

KITCHEN OVERLORD

If you like this book and want to see more geektastic recipes and additional photos of the edible Settlers of Catan boards, visit www.KitchenOverlord.com.

Settlers of the Cold Salad

Geek up your next picnic with this multi-diet-friendly cold salad collection. Everything but the blueberry ocean is vegan. Leave off the rolls and this is also a perfect board for people with Celiac disease or wheat allergies. Primal/paleo dieters can ignore the lentils, but they'll still have three fruit and two vegetable salads to munch on. The whole board is also both Kosher and Halal. No matter what they eat, you can invite all your geek friends to share this picnic.

Hills = 8 cups raspberry balsamic watermelon salad
Forest = 6 cups green bean salad
Pasture = 8 cups green goddess grape and melon salad
Mountains: 6 cups brown lentil salad
Fields = 8 cups cantaloupe, banana and pineapple salad
Desert = 2 cups cold cucumber salad
Ocean = 12 blueberry stuffed sweet rolls

Raspberry Balsamic Watermelon Hills

1 mini/personal watermelon
1/3 cup raspberry balsamic vinegar
2 tbsp brown sugar
1 tsp Kosher salt
¼ tsp ground ginger

Whisk together the vinegar, brown sugar, Kosher salt, and ginger.

While those flavors mingle, cut your personal watermelon in half and attack it's innards with a melon baller. Save on cleanup by dropping the balls directly into the vinegar mix. When you run out of melon, gently toss the balls in the sauce.

You can serve this immediately, but like most cold salads, it tastes even better the next day.

Cold Cucumber Salad Desert

2 cucumbers, peeled and seeded
¼ cup rice wine vinegar
2 cloves garlic, crushed

1 tsp basil
½ tsp salt

Cut your cucumbers in half length-wise. Peel off their skins and use a spoon to gut out the seeds. Cut the remains into thin, C shaped strips.

Mix the rice wine vinegar, crushed garlic, basil, and salt. Dump the cucumbers into the mix and stir until all the slices are well coated.

Green Bean Salad Forest

1 pound fresh green beans
4 garlic cloves, minced
1 tbsp olive oil
1 lemon, juiced and zested
1 tsp Herbes de Provance
1 tsp salt

To avoid overheating your house in summer, instead of steaming or blanching your green beans, go ahead and microwave them until they're crisp-tender. In my microwave, that means about 4 minutes, but your mileage may vary.

While the beans cook, mince the lemon zest. Mix it with the lemon juice, garlic, olive oil salt, and Herbes de Provance. When the green beans are crisp-tender, drown them in ice cold water to preserve their color and texture. Toss your freshly chilled beans in the lemon juice mix until they're thoroughly coated.

Green Goddess Grape and Melon Pasture

1 honeydew melon
2 cups green grapes
3 Granny Smith apples
1 tbsp fresh, chopped mint
1 tbsp honey
1 tbsp rice wine vinegar
pinch Kosher salt
juice of 1 lemon

Start by mixing the honey, vinegar, mint, and salt in a large bowl. Next, core and chop the granny smith apples. Toss them in the fresh lemon juice to preserve color.

Now gut the seeds from your honeydew and use your melon baller on the flesh within. Toss the honedew balls, chopped apples, and otherwise untouched grapes into the honey mix. Give it all a good stir so every piece is coated. This salad is good fresh but tastes even better in four hours.

To make this vegan, substitute 1 tbsp sugar for the honey and increase the rice wine vinegar to 1 ½ tbsp.

Cantaloupe, Banana and Pineapple Salad

1 cantaloupe
1 can chunk pineapple
3 bananas
1 tbsp honey
½ tsp powdered ginger
juice of 1 lime

Drain the pineapple. Retain 1 tbsp of the canned juice. Mix it with the fresh lime juice, honey, and powdered ginger.

By now, you know what that melon baller is for. Transform your cantaloupe from one sphere into countless tiny ones. Throw them in the pineapple juice.

Peel the banana and chop it into chunks roughly the same size as your cantaloupe balls. Finally, add the pineapple.

Give it all a good stir so the pieces are evenly coated in sauce. Unlike the rest of the cold salads, this one needs to be made right before serving. If you leave the bananas in all that citrus overnight, they'll undergo an unwholesome transformation. Don't let bad things happen to good food.

Brown Lentil Mountains

3 cups veggie broth
1 ½ cups brown lentils
1 carrot, finely chopped
½ cup finely chopped onion
1 garlic clove, chopped
2 tbsp red wine vinegar
2 tbsp fresh lemon juice
1 tbsp fresh basil, chopped
salt and pepper to taste

Pour the veggie broth (no lite stuff here - full fat, full salt) into a pan. Add the brown lentils, carrots and garlic. Bring it to a boil, cover, and cook for 30-45 minutes, or until the lentils are tender but not falling apart. While the lentils cook, mix your vinegar, lemon juice, basil, onion, and salt and pepper.

Once the lentils are cooked, drain them, rinse them in cold water, and dump them in the lemon juice mix. Give it all a good stir. Taste, adjust your salt and pepper, and serve. This tastes even better the next day.

Blueberry Stuffed Sweet Roll Desert

Dough:
4 - 4 ½ cups bread flour
1 tbsp yeast
1 ½ cups milk
½ cup sugar
2 eggs
2 tbsp softened butter
1 tsp salt

Filling:
2 cups frozen blueberries
½ cup brown sugar
½ cup melted butter

Glaze:
2 cups powdered sugar
juice of 1 lemon
2 tbsp water
½ tsp blue food coloring

Okay, this breaks the cool, summer trend. If it's any consolation, you can always make these on a cool night (possibly in February) and freeze them until they're needed.

Start by heating the milk until it's the temperature of a warm bath. Mix in the yeast. Let that bloom for 10 minutes.

Add the sugar, salt, eggs and softened butter. Mix it all into a single frothy mess. Now stir in the flour. If you have a stand mixer, attach the dough hook and let it do the hard labor for the next 6-7 minutes. If you're kneading by hand, show that dough who's boss for the next 8-10 minutes.

Once you have achieved a well-kneaded dough, cover it with a clean kitchen towel and let it rise for an hour. When you come back, dust a clean surface with flour, punch down your dough, and roll it into a large rectangle.

Spread the melted butter filling over your dough rectangle. Top that with the brown sugar. Finally, add an even layer of blueberries. Carefully roll the dough along the long side until you now have a long tube of sweet temptation. Cut it into 1 inch slices and arrange them 3 inches apart on a greased cookie sheet. Don't put them any closer. You want big round cinnamon-style rolls, not scrunched in square ones.

Let the rolls rise for another hour. Bake them at 350F for 20-25 minutes, or until the tops are a dark golden brown.

While the rolls bake, make your super easy topping by dumping all the glaze ingredients into a bowl and attacking them with a whisk. If you want it thicker, add more sugar. To make it thinner, add a little more lemon juice. Let the rolls cool before painting them with bright blue glaze.

It's easiest to make these (and the rest of the salads, for that matter) the night before. You'll need 12 rolls to complete the board. The rest are yours. Nothing in the rules says you have to share.

Ports: trade hex shaped blue corn chips for the blueberry stuffed sweet rolls to make the board gluten free; trade white sugar plus ½ tbsp rice wine vinegar for honey to make the salads vegan
Victory Point: fry 4 strips of bacon, chop it fine and add both the bacon and drippings to the green beans or lentils

Waffle Bar Map

Waffle bars are great for a leisurely weekend gaming brunch. It's easy to do all the prep before your guests arrive then safely leave all the ingredients out at room temperature for hours. If you're a really good host, you'll leave a big bowl of batter next to a hot waffle iron and let people make fresh waffles when they're hungry, or just as something to do while waiting on that one slow, calculating player to finally finish their turn.

Hills = 8 cups sliced strawberries
Forest = 8 cups green grapes
Pasture = 6 cups diced green apples (tossed in lemon kuice)
Fields = 6 cups bananas foster
Mountains = 8 cups chocolate chips
Desert = 2 cups whipped cream

Settlers Waffle Batter

2 cups flour
1 cup milk
½ cup buttermilk
4 tbsp butter, melted
2 eggs
2 tbsp sugar
1 tbsp baking powder
1 tsp vanilla extract

Dump all the dry ingredients in a bowl and mix them well. Now add all the wet ingredients. Keep stirring until you achieve a lump-free batter. Ladle your batter onto a piping hot, well lubed waffle iron (seriously, don't forget the cooking spray) and cook until golden brown.

If you've only had waffles from a boxed mix before, it's totally worth the extra five minutes to mix some batter up from scratch. You'll be pleasantly surprised.

Whipped Cream Desert

1 pint heavy whipping cream
1 tsp vanilla extract
¼ cup packed brown sugar
pinch salt

Fresh whipped cream is amazingly easy and always worth it. Just pour everything into a bowl and attack it with a hand mixer until it miraculously transforms from a liquid to a solid. For both a waffle and bananas foster topping, I like to add some extra vanilla and sugar.

If you own a stand mixer, this is even easier. Dump everything into the bowl, hook up your whisk attachment, and just walk away while the frothy magic happens. Or, in this case, go make your bananas foster.

If you don't own a stand mixer, just use a regular hand mixer and admire as your liquids become sweet, tasty solids.

Bananas Foster Fields

3 pounds firm bananas, peeled and sliced
1 stick butter
½ cup brown sugar
¼ cup dark rum
½ tbsp vanilla extract
1 tsp cinnamon
½ tsp Kosher salt

You'll get the best result from stiff yellow bananas that are bordering on green. Darker yellow and spotted bananas are sweeter, but they're also mushier and therefore prone to turning into banana paste if you handle them too much while cooking.

Now that you have your bananas, get out your largest skillet. The bananas want room. Melt the butter over a medium-high heat. Add your sliced bananas. Give them a good stir to make sure all the slices are well coated in butter.

Cook for 3-4 minutes, or until the bottom bananas start to turn a nice golden brown. Give them another good stir, and cook for another 3-4 minutes.

Sprinkle the brown sugar over the bananas. Top that with the cinnamon, Kosher salt, vanilla extract, and dark rum.

Stir it all again until every piece of banana is well coated. Let everything cook down for another 2 minutes, stirring occasionally as a glaze forms.

If you don't want to eat molten, melted plastic, let your bananas foster fields cool somewhat before filling your hex shaped serveware.

Ports: trade strawberries for cherries; trade chocolate chips for blueberries
Year of Plenty: add Nutella and pecans or walnuts
Victory Point: add bacon

Biscuit Bar

This is even more low maintenance than the waffle bar. In fact, as long as you have plenty of table space, you can easily make both as gamer fodder for a brunch-time adventure. Whip up both the butters the night before, bake the biscuits first thing in the morning, and you have a perfectly good edible board that can safely sit out at room temperature through a marathon gaming session.

I used the smaller, ½ cup capacity hex dishes for this edible map because no one needs 8 pounds of compound butter.

Hills = 2 cups sliced strawberries
Forest = 1 ½ cups chopped chives
Pasture = 2 cups herbed compound butter
Fields = 2 cups sliced cheddar cheese
Mountains = 1 ½ cups grape jelly
Desert = ½ cup honey butter

Herbed Hexed Compound Butter

1 cup butter
4 tbsp fresh lemon zest
4 tbsp fresh thyme
4 tbsp fresh basil
2 tsp lime juice
1 tsp coarse Kosher salt
3-4 drops green dye (optional)

Soften your butter. (Leaving it out overnight works just fine.) Chop your lemon zest and herbs. Mix the lime juice and salt into the herbs until well blended. If you literally want greener pastures, add a few drops of green food coloring. Now mix it all into your butter.

To achieve the hex shape, roll your butter into a thick log, a little fatter than your hex shaped cookie cutter. Wrap the log tightly in plastic then put it in the fridge to harden for at least 4 hours. I leave my compound butters in the fridge overnight.

When you're ready to serve, cut the butter into slices a little thinner than the width of your cookie cutter. Lay the butter slices flat and stamp out a hex shape. If you don't have a small hex shaped cookie cutter, gather up a knife and patiently cut each slice into a hex. Either way, you'll have some leftover non-artistically shaped herb butter. I'm sure you can find a use for it.

Home Made Honey Butter

½ cup butter
¼ cup local honey
½ tsp table salt
½ tsp vanilla extract

Simply soften your butter then mix in the honey and salt. It won't taste like store bought honey butter, which is mostly margarine and artificial flavoring. It'll taste better. You can make it into a log like the herb butter or just pile it up in your board's desert hex. If you've never had actual honey butter, you owe it to yourself to give the real thing a try.

Buttermilk Hex Biscuits

2 cups all purpose flour
1 cup buttermilk
¼ cup unsalted butter
1 tsp baking powder
¼ tsp baking soda
1 tsp salt

You can always save some time by cutting store bought tubes of refrigerated biscuit dough into hexes, but the real things are a lot easier than most people think.

Preheat your oven to 450F. While it's heating, mix all your dry ingredients in a bowl.

Get your butter out of the fridge (the colder the better) and cut it into tiny cubes. Either put the butter and flour mix in a food processor or use your fingers to really work the butter into the flour mix. Either way, keep at it until you have a coarse, mealy texture. Finally, add the buttermilk.

Flour a clean surface and knead the dough a few times. This isn't yeast bread. The less you handle it the better.

Roll your biscuit dough into a big rectangle and attack it with your hex shaped cookie cutter. You need at least 12 good looking hex biscuits to fill in the corners of the board. If you're not afraid of a little extra fat, go ahead and brush the surfaces with some melted butter before you put them in the oven.

Bake for 10-12 minutes or until the tops are a light golden brown.

Ports: trade 2 tbsp dried Herbes de Provance for the compound butter's thyme and basil
Year of Plenty: add some of the cheddar and chives to the biscuit dough before baking.
Victory Point: add bacon

Breakfast Taco Map

Depending on where you live and how much tortilla you like, these work equally well as breakfast tacos or breakfast burritos. The only difference between the two is size. Since the Geneva Convention forbids serving three hour old cold scrambled eggs, you should leave out a skillet and butter. There's always one super slow player who takes forever contemplating their next move. Your guests can literally scramble an egg in two minutes and load their tortilla up with their favorite fixings while waiting on their next turn. If serving people with Celiac disease or wheat allergies, make sure to provide gluten free corn tortillas. Paleo or low carb dieters can leave off the tortillas altogether in favor of a breakfast scramble.

Hills = 6 cups salsa
Forest = 8 cups green bell peppers, diced
Pasture = 6 cups guacamole
Mountains = 8 cups ground sausage
Fields = 8 cups shredded mozzarella cheese
Desert = 2 cups diced onions
Ocean = 12 eggs

Salsafied Hills

6 large tomatoes
1 yellow onion
4 cloves garlic
1 lime, juiced
¼ cup cilantro
1 tbsp olive oil
½ tbsp sugar
1 tsp Kosher salt
½ tsp ground cumin
½ tsp chili powder
1 jalapeno pepper, seeded (optional)

I like my salsa smooth and easy. Just dump everything in a food processor and pulse until you reach your desired texture. If you want it chunkier, don't pulse it down into a liquid.

If you want it really chunky, you can always go old school and chop everything up by hand.

Either way, put your final result into a glass bowl, cover it with plastic, and refrigerate for at least 4 hours while the flavors mingle. Leave it overnight and it'll taste even better.

Guacamole Pastures

5 avocados, seeded and peeled
1 tomato
½ yellow onion
2 chilies, seeded
¼ cup cilantro
2 tsp Kosher salt
½ lime, juiced
½ tsp cumin
½ tsp cayenne

Put everything but the avocados into a food processor or blender and pulse until you have a sticky paste. Dump that into a bowl and add your avocado meat.

Use the back of a fork to gently mash the paste into the avocado. You don't want to overwork it. Respect the avocado.

When you're done, squeeze the other half of your lime over the surface to help keep it from turning brown. Let your guacamole sit at room temperature for at least an hour for the flavors to mingle.

Sausage-ish Mountains

2 lbs ground turkey
1 tbsp olive oil
2 cloves garlic, minced
2 tbsp Kosher salt
2 tbsp brown sugar
1 tbsp ground sage
1 tsp fennel seeds
1 tsp marjoram
1 tsp nutmeg
1 tsp black pepper
pinch cloves
pinch red pepper flakes

Modern breakfast sausage is a mess. Most processed sausage has gluten in it as a binder, so it's off limits to people with Celiac disease, wheat allergies, or who are following a primal/paleo diet. A lot of people who have no problems with gluten can't handle the levels of nitrates in processed meat, so breakfast sausage isn't an option for them, either.

Luckily, sausage crumbles are just meat and spices. It's not that hard to whip up a substitute they can all eat.

Put a large skillet over a medium-high heat. Add the olive oil and minced garlic. Gently fry the garlic for 3-4 minutes, or until it barely starts to brown. Add the sage, fennel, marjoram, nutmeg, fresh ground black pepper, cloves, and red pepper flakes. Fry all your spices for another 1-2 minutes. This really brings out the flavor and makes your place smell like a proper breakfast.

Now add the salt and brown sugar. Mix until you have a tasty spice paste. Finally, add the meat and continue mixing until it is well coated with spices. Keep cooking until your ground turkey is cooked all the way through.

Mind you, making gluten free meat sausage leaves the vegetarian, vegan, Kosher, and Halal people out. I recommend buying vegan hamburger crumbles for them. Use the same technique to transform the fake burger meat into fake sausage meat, but add 2 more tbsp olive oil or else the vegan crumbles will burn.

You'll find fake vegan meat in the frozen food section of most grocery stores. The proteins in the vegan meats are all grain based, so you want to make extra sure your gluten free people know which hexes are meaty and which ones are veggie.

Ports: trade vegan "cheez" shreds for the mozzarella
Year of Plenty: add fresh hash browns and black beans
Victory Point: add bacon

Settlers of the Nacho Bar

Nachos are a great pizza substitute. After all, you're still loading up a carby base with sausage, onions, tomatoes, and cheese. A nacho bar is faster than pizza delivery, never gets cold, and since everyone makes their own dish, you don't have to worry about fights over toppings. You can easily make it gluten-free with the right tortilla chips. You can also make it vegetarian, Kosher, and Halal by substituting fake meat for the ground lamb.

Hills = 4 large tomatoes, diced
Forest = 8 jalapenos, diced
Pasture = 8 cups guacamole (from Breakfast Taco map)
Fields = 8 cups shredded cheddar or cheddar jack cheese
Mountains = 6 cups taco meat
Desert = 1 large yellow onion, diced
Ocean = blue corn chips

Taco Mountain Meat

2 lbs ground lamb, ground turkey or vegan crumbles
1 tbsp olive oil
1 tbsp chili powder
1 tbsp Kosher salt
½ tbsp paprika
2 tsp cumin
1 tsp fresh ground black pepper
½ tsp garlic powder
½ tsp onion powder
½ tsp red pepper flakes
¼ tsp oregano

Heat your olive oil in a large skillet over medium heat. Add all the seasonings and mix well. Let them cook together for 1-2 minutes to release the flavors, then add the meat of your choice. If you're using lean ground turkey or vegan crumbles, add an extra tbsp of olive oil. Ground lamb will be plenty fatty.

Cook over medium heat, stirring occasionally, until the meat is cooked all the way through. If you're using vegan crumbles you only need to, cook for 5-6 minutes total, or until the meat substitute is warmed all the way through and well integrated with the seasonings.

If you're not sure which meat option to use, I recommend going with the vegan crumbles since they're perfectly safe left at room temperature all day long. (After all, they're not really meat.)

This means the host can put the board together first thing in the morning and forget about it for the rest of the day since everything is room temperature safe. However, if you're feeding people with gluten sensitivity or who are primal/paleo diners, stick with the turkey or lamb.

Nacho Assembly Instructions

The brand "Food Should Taste Good" makes gluten free hex shaped blue corn tortilla chips. Someone there is obviously a board game nerd. You can find them at schmancy/health food stores like Whole Foods or Sprouts or order them online. It takes 3-4 bags to properly surround an edible game board.

If you aren't worried about gluten, most grocery stores now carry some variety of regular triangle shaped blue corn chips for your simulated edible ocean needs.

I provided players with 8-9 inch round cake pans for individualized nachos, but you can also use cookie or baking sheets.

To make your nachos, lay down a healthy layer of blue corn chips. Add your favorite toppings and sprinkle cheese on top.

Put your nachos 6-8 inches below your broiler and let the cheese melt for the next 1-2 minutes.

Don't be afraid of your broiler. It isn't actually an angry demon that can only win freedom by burning 101 innocent hands. It's a lonely tool just waiting for your loving attention.

That said, being so lonely means it needs constant attention. The difference between perfectly melted cheese with a hint of brown on top and evil blackened dairy is only a few seconds.

If you're using vegan cheese, look for the brands that advertise their meltability. Otherwise, you'll end up with crispy yellow straws.

Ports: trade vegan "cheez" shreds for the cheddar or refried beans for the taco meat
Road Building: add colored bell pepper strips between hexes
Year of Plenty: add diced jalapeno peppers and sour cream
Victory Point: add bacon

Mediterranean Map

This board looks like it took hours, but is actually an easy weeknight meal that can be assembled in about 45 minutes. Get your keema started first. While that's cooking, go ahead and experiment with making hummus from scratch. It takes less than 5 minutes. The tzatziki and cucumber salad only take longer because of the chopping. You'll have all the sides ready by the time the main dish finishes cooking. Plus, your place will smell amazing.

In the spirit of Settlers, I used lamb. However, you can make the entire board vegan by substituting vegan crumbles for the lamb and soy yogurt for the dairy. That also makes the entire board Kosher and Halal. Merely substituting soy for cow dairy makes it safe for lactose-intolerant gamers. For your Celiac friends, everything but the pita is gluten free.

Hills = 6 cups roasted red pepper hummus
Forest = 6 cups cucumber salad
Pasture = 8 cups keema
Mountains = 8 cups dried black mission figs and/or raisins
Fields = 1 bag pita bread, cut into triangles
Desert = 2 cups tzatziki

Roasted Red Bell Pepper Hummus Hills

4 (15 oz) cans chick peas, drained
1 1/2 cup roasted red bell peppers, drained
½ cup tahini
6 garlic cloves
4 tbsp olive oil
1 tsp dried basil
1 tsp salt
Juice of 4 lemons

Hummus is almost embarrassingly easy.

Put everything in a food processor. Let it majestically whir until all the solids are transformed into paste. You'll need to scrape down the sides a couple times, but that's the only work involved. If you'd like your hills a little redder, feel free to add a few drops of red food coloring. You can also make slightly chunkier hummus by dumping everything in a blender.

Cucumber Salad Forests

2 large cucumbers
1 bunch mint leaves
2 tbsp lemon juice
2 tbsp olive oil
1 tbsp sugar

Cut your cucumber length-wise. Use a spoon to fish out the seedy cucumber guts. Cut the remainder into C shaped slices.

Mix the lemon juice, olive oil, sugar, and optionally, a pinch each of salt and pepper. If you want your forest leafy, mince up the mint and add it to the mix. If you prefer a more subtle effect, bruise your mint leaves and use them to line the bottom of your serve ware.

(Mine came out so subtle you can't even see them. I recommend arranging the mint along the sides as well as the bottom so it looks like your forest has leaves.)

Add the cucumber slices to your lemon juice mix and stir until all of the cucumber is well coated. Ideally, let it sit at room temperature for at least half an hour before serving to let the flavors soak in.

Keema Pastures

2 lbs lean ground lamb
1 large white onion, minced
1 cup frozen green peas
1 tbsp olive oil
1 tbsp garam masala
2 tsp Kosher salt
1 tsp ground cumin
1 tsp turmeric
1 tsp chili powder
4 cloves garlic, crushed
1 inch knob peeled ginger, chopped fine
1 cup plain yogurt or plain soy yogurt
Juice of 1 lime

In a large skillet, heat the oil to medium-high.

Add your onion, garlic, and ginger. Fry until the onion just barely starts to brown. Add the turmeric, garam masala, and chili powder. Mix well, then keep frying the spices for another 2 minutes.

Add the ground meat. Mix it into the seasonings until every scrap is thoroughly coated. Cook until the meat is completely browned.

Add in the frozen peas and keep cooking until they are restored to a warm state of edibility. Squeeze in the lime juice and give it all one more good stir.

If you like yogurt (and no one you're serving is lactose intolerant), mix in a cup of it. This adds a great, creamy texture.

Tzatziki Desert

1 cucumber, chopped fine
1 cup Greek yogurt
2 garlic cloves, crushed
1 tbsp fresh chopped mint
1 tbsp fresh lemon juice
½ tbsp olive oil
1 tsp salt

Mix everything in a bowl.

Yes, it really is that simple. Since this is supposed to be a desert, you could complicate things by first peeling and seeding the cucumber so it won't add so much green to the board, but I like my tzatziki with a little texture.

Ports: trade ground lamb for ground vegan crumbles and trade cow yogurt for soy or coconut milk yogurt to make this an entirely vegan board
Year of Plenty: add pitted dates stuffed with almonds or mascarpone cheese
Road Building: add sliced carrots and bell peppers along the hex borders

All American Meatloaf Map

Old fashioned American comfort food happens to come in perfect colors for a Settlers game board. The meatloaf takes some time to cook, but the rest of the side dishes make up for it by being as fast and easy as they are tasty.

Hills = 8 cups tomatoes
Forest = 2 large bunches asparagus
Pasture = 8 cups frozen green peas
Mountains = meatloaf
Fields = 8 cups sweet corn
Desert = biscuits

Meatloaf Mountains

2 pounds lean ground beef
1 ½ cups Italian seasoned bread crumbs
1 egg
1 onion, chopped
1 green bell pepper, diced
4 cloves garlic, crushed
1 cup diced tomatoes, drained
4 tbsp tomato paste
2 tbsp brown sugar
1 tsp salt
1 tsp pepper
1 cup ketchup

Preheat your oven to 375. While it's heating up, mix the tomato paste, brown sugar, salt and pepper in a huge bowl. Now throw in everything but the ketchup and knead it until you achieve a harmonious meaty mass. If it's too wet, add another quarter cup of bread crumbs.

Put the lump of meat in a glass baking dish and shape it into a round dome of meat. Flatten it out on top. Make sure the meat has at least 2 inches of open space between it and the edge of the pan. Don't succumb to the temptation to put it in a loaf pan or else you'll end up with a tiny wad of meat swimming in a sea of juices.

You need space for the juice to run off. Pour the ketchup on top.

Tent some aluminum foil over the meatloaf. Bake for 40 minutes. Remove the foil and bake for another 30 minutes. Take it out of the oven, drain off the juices, and let it cool for at least 20 minutes before cutting or else it will completely fall apart on you.

Use your largest hex shaped cookie cutter to make big, meaty slices. Sneak the rest into a less artistic but equally tasty serving bowl set off to one side.

If you're serving people with Celiac disease, gluten allergies, or who are primal/paleo dieters, substitute 1 cup of almond meal for the seasoned bread crumbs and add 1 tbsp Italian seasoning. Since a lot of commercial ketchup has gluten, mix 4 tbsp Italian seasoned tomato paste with 1 tsp apple cider vinegar and 4 tbsp water. Spread that over the top of the meatloaf instead of ketchup.

Clove and Honey Pea Pastures

8 cups frozen peas
4 tbsp honey
4 tbsp butter
1 tbsp Kosher salt
8 whole cloves

Mix everything in a large, microwave safe bowl. Irradiate it until your peas are warmed through and your honey becomes a liquid. My microwave took about 5 minutes, but due to wattage, yours may vary. Stir every

2 minutes and check the temperature. To maximize flavor, leave the cloves in until right before serving.

Garlic Butter Asparagus Forests

2 bunches asparagus
8 cloves garlic, crushed
4 tbsp butter
½ tsp salt

Melt the butter in a large skillet over medium-high heat. Add the garlic and salt. Cook for 3-4 minutes, so the garlic has a chance to flavor the butter. Add the asparagus, mix until it's well coated in butter, and cover. Cook for 8-10 minutes, stirring occasionally, until the asparagus is crisp-tender.

Sweet Corn Fields

8 cups of corn
8 tbsp butter
4 tbsp honey
2 tsp Kosher salt

I freely admit that I'm a corn snob. Fresh corn on the cob is infinitely better than canned. Canned is notably better than frozen. Frozen isn't actually food.

If corn on the cob is in season, you'll need about 8-10 ears depending on size. Shuck the corn, bring a big pot of water to a boil, and throw in the ears. Put a lid on the pot and turn off the heat. Let it sit undisturbed for 15

minutes. Strain it, rinse it in cool water, and let it rest and cool for a few minutes before cutting the beautifully crisp kernels off the ears. Or, y'know, drain some cans.

However you acquire your kernels, you now want to mix them with some delicious sauce. You can skip some time by just using the same garlic butter sauce as the asparagus.

However, if you want to give each side dish an individual buttery spin, melt the honey and butter in a large, microwave safe bowl. That takes about 20 seconds, one good stir, and 20 more seconds in my microwave, but your wattage may vary. Add the salt and stir it one more time. Now dump in all those kernels and mix until they're coated in sweet deliciousness.

Tomato Hills

If you're feeling fancy, use the Grilled Rosemary and Cherry Tomato Road recipe from the Building Costs chapter. You can also serve sliced tomatoes with a bit of salt and pepper on top to eat with the meatloaf or plain cherry tomatoes as a hilly side dish.

Biscuit Desert

Use the biscuit recipe from the Biscuit Board. If you're pinched for time, you can always buy some pre-made biscuits from the grocery store. I won't judge you.

Ports: trade the tomatoes for roasted red peppers or trade the asparagus for green beans
Year of Plenty: add anywhere from 1 tsp to 2 tbsp Sriracha to the meatloaf if you like it hot
Victory Point: add 6 slices chopped, cooked bacon to the meatloaf

Deconstructed Salad Nicoise

This dramatic French salad is meant to be served at room temperature and enjoyed over a long, leisurely lunch. That makes it perfect fodder for a health conscious crowd of gamers. It's also the most obscure-diet-friendly board in this book since it is already gluten free and can be served as-is to people who keep Kosher and Halal. Vegetarians can ignore the tuna hexes, primal/paleo dieters can avoid the potatoes, and you can invite all your friends over to share one big meal.

Hills = 6 cups cherry tomatoes
Forest = 3 lbs green beans
Pasture = 1 head iceberg lettuce
Mountains = 4 lbs baby red potatoes
Fields = 4 large pouches or medium cans tuna
Desert = 8-12 hard boiled eggs

Technique

Cut your red skinned potatoes into equal sized pieces. Dump them in a gallon of boiling water. Add a pinch of salt and let them cook for 5-8 minutes, or until tender. Use a slotted spoon to fish out your potatoes. Rinse them under cold water to stop the cooking and set the potatoes aside.

You can now either dump out your potato water and start from scratch or reuse it to cook your green beans. I'm a fan of efficiency. Either way, put your fresh green beans in some boiling water and let them cook until they're tender-crisp, about 4-5 minutes. While they're cooking, fill a large bowl with ice water. When your beans are ready, use a slotted spoon to transfer them from the boiling water to their icy bath. This stops the cooking (so they don't end up too mushy) and preserves their color.

Use the largest, prettiest lettuce leaves to make liners for your tuna mountains. In France, canned tuna is the norm, but you're welcome to pan sear fresh tuna if that's in your budget. A full can or pouch of tuna won't quite fill a hex, so fluff it up with extra lettuce before arranging your tuna on top.

After that, simply fill the rest of the hexes with their appropriate edible terrain. Drizzle everything with your freshly made dressing. This is already a massive amount of food, but feel free to enhance the continental atmosphere by adding on a store bought crusty baguette and the herb butter from the biscuit bar.

Salad Nicoise Dressing

½ cup olive oil
1 shallot, minced fine
1 lemon, juiced
2 tbsp basil
1 tbsp thyme
½ tbsp dark Dijon mustard
1tsp Kosher salt
½ tsp fresh ground black or mixed peppercorns

Simply pour everything into a large bowl and whisk it together. This board makes a dramatic amount of salad (remember, each hex holds 2 cups of food) so feel free to double the recipe if you like your salads heavily dressed.

Ports: substitute cooked seitan strips for the tuna to make the board vegan or cooked sweet potatoes for the red potatoes to make the board primal
Year of Plenty: add ½ cup olives, ½ cup anchovy filets, or ½ cup caper berries

Fish Fry Board

I love a good, southern fish fry. At first glance, the green beans, broccoli slaw, and lemon slices make this board look deceptively healthy, but those potatoes are drowning in delicious butter and the well drained fish spent just the right amount of time in the fryer. It's equally good for a Catholic meatless Friday, Kosher dairy meal (fish is considered parve, which means "neutral"), or anyone who loves crispy fried fish with all the fixings.

Hills = 8 cups red skinned potatoes
Forest = 6 cups green beans
Pasture = 8 cups broccoli slaw
Mountains = 8 cups fried fish
Fields = 6-8 lemons, sliced into wedges
Desert = 2 cups tartar sauce
Bread = 12 garlic and herb filled pull apart rolls

Mountains of Beer Battered Fried Fish

3 lbs firm white fish filets (such as cod, halibut, or walleye)
2 cups flour
¼ cup cornstarch
2 cups ice cold beer
2 eggs, separated
1 tsp salt
½ gallon oil

Preheat your oil to 400 degrees. While it's heating, cut your fish into triangles. This makes the filets easier to arrange in the hexes.

Mix your flour, cornstarch and salt in one bowl. In another bowl, mix your egg yolks and cold beer until they're well blended. In a third bowl, beat your egg whites until they're stiff. If you skip this step and dump whole eggs into the batter, you'll end up with a thick, heavy, oily crust. The cold beer and beaten egg whites keep it nice and fluffy.

Mix the wet ingredients into the dry ones. When they're well blended, but still a little lumpy, fold in the egg whites.

Now you need to work fast before your light batter turns to a heavy paste. Dip a wedge of fish in the batter and swirl it around until well coated, then drop it in the hot oil. Fry a few pieces at a time (they shouldn't touch) for about 4 minutes each. Use a metal slotted spoon to pull them out before arranging them on a nice layer of paper towels to drain. Repeat the process until you run out of fish.

Garlic and Lemon Red Skinned Potatoes Hills and Green Beans Forests

4 pounds red skinned potatoes
4 large lemons, juiced
4 cloves garlic, minced
4 tbsp butter
1 tsp Kosher salt

Cut your red skinned potatoes into equal sized pieces. Dump them in a gallon of boiling water. Add a pinch of salt and let them cook for 5-8 minutes, or until tender. Drain.

While the potatoes cook, melt the butter in a skillet over medium-high heat. Add the minced garlic and Kosher salt. Sautee the garlic in the butter, stirring frequently, for about five minutes. Finish it with the fresh squeezed lemon juice.

Remove your sauce from the heat. Pour about half of it in a bowl and set it aside. Add the drained potatoes to the skillet and toss them in the remaining sauce until all your hills are alive with the taste of garlic.

If you have limited pans, reuse your potato water to cook your green beans. Boil them for 4-5 minutes or until they're tender-crisp. Dump them in a big bowl of ice water to stop the cooking and preserve the color. Serve the green beans with the remaining garlic butter sauce.

Broccoli Slaw Pastures

2 16-oz bags premixed broccoli slaw
½ cup rice wine vinegar
1 tbsp brown sugar
1 tbsp soy sauce
1/2 tsp sesame oil
2 garlic cloves, minced
1 tsp ginger paste (or ½ tsp powdered ginger)
1 tsp sweet chili paste

Put everything but the slaw mix in a large bowl and whisk it all together. Add the slaw mix and stir until all the veggies are coated in dressing. This recipe works just as well with cabbage based coleslaw.

Tartar Sauce Desert

1 ½ cup mayonnaise
¼ cup pickle relish
1 tbsp white vinegar
1 scallion or ¼ cup onion, finely chopped
1 tsp Dijon mustard
1 tsp Kosher salt
½ tsp fresh ground pepper

Simply dump everything in a bowl and mix it up until you have a familiar, slightly lumpy white paste. Keep it in the fridge until you're ready to assemble the board.

Feel free to make it a night or two in advance. The longer the flavors mingle, the better the sauce.

Garlic and Herb Filled Pull-Apart Rolls

3 - 3 ½ cups flour
1 tbsp yeast
1 tbsp sugar
¾ cup water
¾ cup milk
6 tbsp melted butter
8 cloves garlic, finely minced
1 tbsp chopped basil (or 1 tsp dried)
½ tbsp chopped thyme (or ½ tsp dried)
½ tbsp Kosher salt

Dissolve your yeast and sugar in ¾ cup warm water. Walk away for 10 minutes while the yeast blooms. When you come back, add the milk and 2 cups of flour. Mix that into a nice, thick paste, then add 2 tbsp of the butter. Keep adding flour until your paste transforms into a dough.

If you have a stand mixer, attach the dough hook and let it claw away at your bread for about 6 minutes. If you're working by hand, knead the dough for 8-10 minutes. Cover with a clean dishcloth and let rise for the next hour, or until doubled in size.

While you're waiting, melt the other 4 tbsp of butter in a skillet over medium-high heat. Add the finely chopped garlic and let it cook for 6-7 minutes, or until the garlic just barely starts to brown. Add your herbs and salt, then cook for another minute, stirring frequently. Remove from the heat.

Once your dough has doubled, dust a clean surface with flour. Punch down the dough and roll it into a large rectangle. Paint the rectangle with your herb butter mix.

Cut the rectangle into eight evenly sized pieces and stack them on top of one another, butter side up. Put your last piece on butter side down. Now use your hands to press the dough down into a block.

Roll it into another rectangle, then roll that rectangle up like a jelly roll. You have now created tons of tasty layers.

Lube up a couple muffin tins. Cut two inch slices off the roll of dough and put one in each muffin slot. Let the dough rise for another hour.

Bake at 350F for 12-14 minutes, or until the tops are golden brown.

Feel free to paint the rolls with extra butter before baking for even more fatty deliciousness.

Ports: trade broccoli slaw for traditional mayo based coleslaw; trade pull-apart rolls for gluten free cornbread from the southern board

Year of Plenty: add sweet corn recipe from the meatloaf board and your favorite Mac and Cheese

Robber: steal sweet chili paste from the broccoli slaw recipe

Quick Bread Board

If you're feeling extra ambitious, this is the most playable of all the edible boards. Add some sliced carrots, celery, red and green peppers for the roads, substitute a hex full of hummus for the white bread desert, and just wipe off your numbers, settlements and cities after the game. No fair eating a territory to prevent other players from capturing it. Best of all, the whole board is vegetarian, Kosher, Halal, and tasty.

Hills = maraschino cherry bread
Forest = basil pesto garlic bread
Pasture = jalapeno cornbread
Mountains = hazelnut crusted chocolate bread
Fields = banana bread
Desert = whatever white bread you have on hand

Maraschino Cherry Hills

1 ¾ cups flour
4 tbsp softened butter
2 eggs
1 tsp vanilla
½ cup white sugar
½ cup maraschino cherry juice
½ cup maraschino cherries, roughly chopped
1 tsp baking powder
½ tsp salt

Mix the butter, sugar, eggs, vanilla, and maraschino cherry juice until you have a nice, wet paste. Add the rest of the ingredients. Keep mixing until your batter is free from lumps. Pour it into a thoroughly buttered 9 inch round cake pan and bake at 350F for 35-40 minutes, or until a toothpick stuck in the center comes out clean.

Let the bread cool completely before cutting. If you buttered the pan well enough, you should have no trouble simply pressing a medium hex shaped cookie cutter into it and coming out with a clean piece of bread. I got 4 equal sized hexes and a pile of odd sized tasty scraps from each cake pan. The entire board should fit nicely on a single 15 inch pizza pan.

Basil Pesto Garlic Forests

2 ¼ cups flour
4 tbsp basil pesto
4 cloves minced garlic
2 eggs
1 ½ tsp baking powder
½ tsp Kosher salt
½ cup water
2 tbsp olive oil
4 drops green food coloring

Dump everything in a big bowl and mix until you have a lump-free batter.

Pour your batter into a buttered 9 inch cake pan. Bake it at 350F for 35-40 minutes, or until a toothpick inserted in the center comes out clean. Let it cool, cut it into hexes, and save the scraps for your next pasta dinner.

Jalapeno Cornbread Pastures

1 cup fine ground yellow cornmeal
1 cup flour
1 1/4 cups milk
¼ cup sugar
5 tbsp softened butter
1 ½ tsp baking powder
1 tsp salt
2 eggs
1 4 oz can diced jalapenos with juice

Mix all your dry ingredients. Add in 2 tbsp softened butter plus all your wet ingredients and keep mixing until you have a nice, dense batter.

No kidding around this time. Use at least 1 tbsp of butter to grease your 9 inch round cake pan. Pour in the cornbread batter. Bake at 425F for 20-25 minutes, or until a toothpick inserted in the center comes out clean. While the cornbread is piping hot, spread your remaining butter on the surface.

Let the cornbread cool completely before cutting it into hexes. If you're not a fan of jalapenos, try substituting a can of diced mild green chilies instead.

Hazelnut Crusted Chocolate Mountains

1 ½ cups crushed hazelnuts
1 ½ cups flour
½ cup unsweetened cocoa powder
½ cup white sugar
1 ½ tsp baking powder
½ cup chocolate chips
½ tsp salt
¾ cup milk
1/3 cup canola oil
2 eggs

Mix your flour, cocoa powder, sugar, baking powder, and salt. Add your milk, oil and eggs. Beat well, until you have a smooth batter. Fold in the chocolate chips.

Generously grease a 9 inch round cake pan with more oil or butter. Pour in the batter. Sprinkle a thick layer of crushed hazelnuts on top. Bake at 350F for 30-35 minutes, or until a toothpick inserted in the center comes out clean.

Since these are your mountains, the loaf should bake up taller than your other breads.

Banana Bread Fields

3 ripe bananas, mashed
2 cups flour
½ cup white sugar
½ cup brown sugar
2 tbsp softened butter
1 egg
2 tsp vanilla
1 tsp baking powder
½ tsp salt

Mix your mashed bananas, white sugar, butter, vanilla, egg, and salt until nice and creamy. Add the flour and baking powder and keep mixing until it transforms into batter.

Coat a 9 inch baking pan with butter. This is extra important because without the butter, this recipe is notorious for sticking. Pour in the batter. Sprinkle your brown sugar on top. Bake at 350F for 30-35 minutes, or until a toothpick inserted in the center comes out clean.

Barbecue Board

I've spent enough time in the south and in plains states that I crave super sweet Kings Hawaiian Rolls with barbeque. I don't know how the tradition of serving them together started, but I'm glad it spread.

This board offers a tasty compromise for diverse diets. Everything except the store bought bread is dairy-free. The Kosher, Halal, and vegetarian crowd can eat everything but the chicken. Gluten free folks can eat everything but the pasta salad and rolls.

Hills = 8 cups pulled chicken barbecue
Forest = 8 cups pesto pasta salad
Pasture = 8 cups coleslaw
Mountains = 6 cups vegetarian baked beans
Fields = 6 cups potato salad (use the
Desert = 12 King's Hawaiian Rolls

Pulled Chicken Barbecue Hills

2 pounds boneless, skinless chicken breasts
1 yellow onion, halved and sliced thin
1 tbsp sweet paprika
½ tsp salt
¼ cup water
1 16 oz bottle your favorite barbecue sauce

This is my super lazy recipe for fast barbecue chicken. You can dump it in a crockpot first thing Sunday morning and have a hot, cooked lunch waiting for you with next to no work.

Start by peeling your onion. Cut it in half, slice it thin, and spread the pieces around the bottom of a crockpot. Pour the water on top of the onions.

Mix the paprika with the salt then rub it on your chicken breasts. Arrange the breasts on top of the onions. Cook on low for 4 hours.

When you come back, the chicken should be so tender it falls apart at your touch. Attack the chicken with a large fork. Really get in there and mix it up. The chicken will magically shred. Add just enough of your favorite barbecue sauce to moisten the chicken.

Pesto Pasta Salad Forest

½ pound whole wheat spiral pasta
½ pound regular spiral pasta
½ pound spinach spiral pasta
1 cup fresh basil
½ cup fresh spinach
4 cloves garlic
4 tbsp pine nuts
1 cup olive oil
1 cup parmesan cheese
1 tsp Kosher salt
1 tsp fresh ground black pepper
4-6 drops green food coloring

Boil your pastas according to package directions. (Honestly, I just boiled them all together.)

While your pasta is boiling, put your basil, spinach, garlic, pine nuts, olive oil, salt, pepper, and food coloring in a food processor. Pulse until all your solids are magically transformed into a relatively smooth paste.

When the pasta is cooked and drained, mix it with the pesto sauce. If you're a little less obsessed with color coordinating your board, leave off the green food coloring.

Potato Salad Fields

3 pounds yellow potatoes
1 small yellow onion, chopped
1 stalk celery, diced
1 ¼ cups mayonnaise
½ cup pickle relish
1 tbsp yellow mustard
1 tsp salt
1 tsp fresh ground pepper
6 hard boiled eggs

Cut the potatoes into evenly sized cubes. Traditionally, you'll peel them first, but I like the texture of yellow potato peels. It's entirely up to you. Naked or not, put your cut potatoes into a large pot and cover them with water. Add a pinch of salt. Bring the water to a boil, cover, and reduce the heat to a simmer. Let the potatoes cook 15-18 minutes or until tender. Drain and rinse in cold water.

Meanwhile, dump the chopped onion, diced celery, mayonnaise, pickle relish, mustard, salt, and pepper into a large bowl. Mix it all into a thick paste. Peel and roughly chop the eggs. Go ahead and mix them into the dressing.

When the potatoes are drained and rinsed, add their carby goodness to the party in your bowl. Gently fold them in so everything is well coated without the potatoes breaking up into little pieces. Feel free to make this a day or two in advance. The flavor improves significantly when left overnight.

Coleslaw Pasture

1 head green cabbage
½ cup mayonnaise
¼ cup apple cider vinegar
1 tsp Dijon mustard
½ tbsp sugar
1 tsp salt
1 tsp fresh ground pepper
½ tsp celery seeds
3-4 drops green food coloring (optional)

Attack your cabbage with a chef's knife. Keep chopping until the whole head looks like it was put through a paper shredder. If you've had a bad day, this can be surprisingly cathartic.

Dump everything else in a bowl. Mix it all into a nice, uniform paste. Add the cabbage. Keep mixing until the cabbage is well coated. That's it. Coleslaw is really easy.

Ports: trade the pulled chicken barbeque for barbeque flavored seitan to make the board vegetarian, also substitute vegan mayo in the pasta and potato salads to make the whole thing vegan; substitute asparagus for pasta salad for more gluten free and paleo/primal options
Year of Plenty: add peas and fresh pine nuts to the finished pasta
Robber: steal all the green food coloring

Vegetarian Southern Map

I learned to make both collard greens and red beans from southern woman named Intisar who converted to Islam. I was pleased to learn it only takes a couple minor modifications to make a deliciously unhealthy traditional southern spread entirely vegetarian, Halal, Kosher, and gluten free all at once. No matter where you live or what tradition you come from, people love good food.

Hills = 4 cups red beans and 5 cups rice
Forest = 6 cups collard greens
Pasture = 8 cups fried okra
Mountains = 8 cups smoked sausage cut into coins
Fields = 6 cups fried apples
Desert = 2 cups potato salad (use the recipe from the BBQ board)
Bread = 12 hexes of jalapeno cornbread

Southern Fried Apple Fields

4 pounds granny smith apples
½ cup butter (or vegan butter substitute)
½ cup brown sugar
1 tbsp cinnamon
pinch salt

Peel and core the apples before slicing them thin.

Melt half a cup of butter in a large skillet. Add the sliced apples and stir until they're completely coated in buttery goodness.

Cook over medium-high heat for about 10 minutes, or until the apples start to turn soft. Sprinkle on the pinch of salt, cinnamon, and brown sugar. Mix until everything is well coated and continue cooking for another 5-10 minutes or until the apples reach your preferred softness.

Vegetarian Red Beans and Rice Hills

2 cans red kidney beans, drained
1 can diced tomatoes with juice
1 cup veggie broth
1 medium yellow onion, chopped
4 cloves garlic, minced
2 tbsp olive oil
2 tbsp sugar
½ tbsp paprika
1 tsp nutmeg
1 tsp cinnamon
4 whole cloves
1 bay leaf
5 cups fully cooked rice

Heat the olive oil in a saucepan over medium heat. Add the onion and garlic. Sautee until the onions turn translucent. Add the paprika, nutmeg, cinnamon, and cloves. Give it all a good stir and cook the spices for another 2-3 minutes. Add the bay leaf and veggie broth and bring it to a boil.

Cover the pan, turn the heat down to low, and let it simmer for the next 10 minutes to really bring out the flavor of the spices. Add the sugar and can of diced tomatoes. Stir until everything is well blended. Bring the heat back to a boil and add the red beans. Gently stir the beans so they're well coated. Be careful not to break them apart. Turn the heat down to low and let the beans cook, uncovered, until most of the moisture has evaporated.

To serve, add 1 ¼ cups of rice to a hex, use your fist to make a well in the center, and top it off with 1 cup of red beans. Leave a nice border of rice around the edge for effect.

Pork Free Collard Green Forests

1 head collard greens
1 tbsp apple cider vinegar
4 cups veggie broth
2 cloves garlic, minced
1 red onion, sliced
1 ½ tsp smoked paprika
2 tbsp olive oil
2 tbsp butter
1 tsp Kosher salt
1 tsp fresh ground black pepper
1 bay leaf

Collard greens without bacon may seem like sacrilege to some, but the smoked paprika goes a long way towards restoring that earthy, meaty flavor. Don't substitute sweet or Hungarian paprika. You need the smoke.

Heat your olive oil in a stock pot over medium high heat. Add the onion and sauté for 4-5 minutes. Throw the garlic in there with it and continue cooking for another 4-5 minutes or until the garlic just starts to brown. Add everything but the collard greens themselves and bring the pot to a boil.

While you're waiting, thoroughly rinse and clean the collard greens. Cut off the tough bottoms. Use a small, sharp knife to cut away the thick central stems. Roughly chop the remaining leaves.

Once your broth mix comes to a boil, add the chopped collard greens. Turn the heat down to medium-low and cook for the next 30-45 minutes, stirring occasionally, until the leaves are tender and there is scant moisture left in the pan.

Gluten Free Fried Okra Pastures

2 pounds fresh or frozen okra
6 cups peanut (or other frying) oil
¾ cup cornmeal
¼ cup rice flour
1 tsp Kosher salt
½ tsp fresh ground black pepper
½ tsp garlic powder
½ tsp onion powder
Pinch cayenne pepper
½ cup buttermilk (or ½ cup plain almond milk with 1 tbsp apple cider vinegar)

Start by cutting the stems and ends off your okra then slice it into ½ inch chunks. Soak the okra chunks in buttermilk. If you're using fresh okra, it'll be surprisingly sticky. That's okay. The sap helps keep the batter from falling off while frying.

While the okra soaks, heat your oil to 350F in a stock pot. Go ahead and mix up the cornmeal, rice flour, salt, pepper, garlic, onion, and cayenne into a nice crunchy dry batter.

When the oil is ready, roll a handful of okra in the cornmeal mix and drop it in the hot oil. Don't overcrowd the pan. Okra turns out best when cooked in small batches where each piece gets to float free. Fry the okra for 4-6 minutes or until golden brown. Immediately put it on a thick stack of paper towels to drain. Otherwise, you risk the horror of soggy okra. When deep fried and quickly drained, okra is crispy, light, and surprisingly tasty. If you're not worried about gluten, substitute in ½ cup regular flour for the ¼ cup rice flour.

Sweet Gluten Free Jalapeno Cornbread

Dough:
3 cups yellow cornmeal
1 cup rice flour
1 cup buttermilk
½ cup melted butter
4 eggs
½ cup sugar
2 tsp salt
2 tsp baking powder
1 4-oz can jalapenos with fluid
½ cup yellow corn kernels

Topping:
¼ cup butter
¼ cup honey
pinch Kosher salt

Preheat your oven to 400 degrees.

Grease up a 9x11 cake pan with copious amounts of butter.

Mix the cornmeal, rice flour, sugar, salt, and baking powder. Pretend you're building a city with those two grains. Your three liquid ores are the melted butter, buttermilk, and eggs. Whisk them together and add them to the flours. Once you've achieved a thick batter, mix in the jalapenos and corn kernels.

Spread the mix in your cake pan. Bake for 15-20 minutes, or until a toothpick inserted in the middle comes out clean. While the cornbread bakes, prepare the topping by simply melting your honey, butter, and pinch of salt in the microwave until you achieve a delicious, fatty liquid. As soon as the cornbread comes out of the oven, use a pastry brush to spread the honey butter on top.

Let the cornbread cool completely before carefully using your hex cookie cutter to make a dozen pieces for the board.

Smoked Sausage Mountains

You'll need to customize your smoked sausage based on your dietary needs. Most larger supermarkets or Whole Foods/schmancy grocers carry ropes of both gluten free and vegetarian smoked sausage. If you're in a larger urban market, you might even be able to get your Kosher or Halal versions without needing to order online.

Grocery brands Hilshire Farms, Jenni-O, and Hormel all make gluten free chicken or turkey smoked sausages.

Field Roast, Lightlife and Vivera all make vegetarian smoked sausages.

Pick whichever one fits a majority of your guests.

Ports: trade green beans for collard greens; trade corn or peas for fried okra
Year of Plenty: add a shot of bourbon to the fried apples

Pasta Board

This highly customizable board lets your guests decide what kind of pasta they want for dinner. Simply grab a hex of marinara, pesto, or garlic butter, dump it on your noodles, and top off your meal with the meat or veggie of your choice.

I used the smaller, ½ cup capacity hex dishes for this edible map. Each hex holds a single serving of sauce. If your guests want to sample the whole board, I recommend starting with the garlic butter, moving on to the marinara, and finishing with the pesto.

Hills = Marinara sauce
Forest = 1 lb steamed broccoli
Pasture = pesto sauce
Mountains = 1 lb cooked, roast chicken slices
Fields = garlic butter sauce
Desert = Alfredo sauce

Garlic Butter Fields

1 cup butter
10 cloves garlic, crushed
1 tsp Kosher salt

Heat 2 tbsp of butter in a small saucepan. Add the salt and crushed garlic cloves. Cook until the garlic barely starts to brown, stirring frequently. Add rest of the butter and melt it over a medium heat. When the butter is melted, reduce the heat to low. Cover and let simmer for half an hour, stirring a couple times. Strain out the garlic cloves. You should end up with a lovely, golden, butter sauce with a rich garlic flavor.

If you use too much heat you'll end up with a nutty, dark, browned butter sauce. Its' still tasty, but isn't golden yellow. If that's the case, just tell people your fields are suffering from a drought.

Pesto Pastures

2 cups packed fresh basil leaves
4 cloves garlic
1/3 cup pine nuts
2/3 cup olive oil
1 tsp Kosher salt
½ tsp fresh ground black pepper
½ cup freshly grated Parmesan cheese
Kosher salt and freshly ground black pepper, to taste

Toss your basil leaves, garlic, and pine nuts in a food processor and pulse until they become a smooth paste. Add the salt, pepper, olive oil and cheese and keep pulsing until the paste is transformed into a sauce. If your pesto is too thick, add more olive oil to thin it out before serving.

Alfredo Desert

1 cup cream cheese
½ cup butter
½ cup half and half
½ cup Parmesan cheese
2 cloves garlic, minced
1 tsp Kosher salt
1 tsp fresh ground black pepper

Fresh Alfredo sauce is as easy as it is impressive.

Melt the butter in a medium saucepan. Cut the cream cheese into cubes and drop it in the melted butter. Stir it up until the cream cheese is also melted. Add the Parmesan, garlic, salt, and pepper. Keep stirring until the cheese is melted. Turn off the heat and add the half and half. Stir some more until the sauce is a thick pool of dairy goodness. If it's too thick, add another 1-2 tbsp half and half.

Take the saucepan off the heat and let it sit for 5 minutes to both cool and thicken up.

Basil Marinara Hills

¼ cup fresh basil leaves
¼ cup olive oil
½ cup white wine
2 14.5 oz cans stewed tomatoes
6 oz can tomato paste
½ small onion, chopped
4 garlic cloves, crushed
1 tsp thyme
1 tsp salt
1 tsp fresh ground mixed peppercorns

Bring the olive oil to a medium-high heat in a large saucepan. Add the chopped onion and crushed garlic. Cook for 6-8 minutes, stirring occasionally, or until the garlic starts to brown.

Put everything else in your food processor. Once the onions and garlic have cooked, scoop those in there too. Let it whir away until you have a smooth sauce.

Dump the Marinara back in your sauce pan and bring it to a boil. Cover, reduce the heat to low, and let simmer for half an hour while the flavors mingle.

Ports: trade regular pasta for gluten free pasta; trade broccoli for honey clove peas from the Meatloaf Board
Year of Plenty: add toasted pine nuts, sliced button mushrooms, cherry tomatoes, or cheese
Road Building: add roasted red bell peppers and julienned carrots to the ridges between hexes
Victory Point: add bacon

Roasted Root Vegetable Board

To make this hearty autumn carb-fest easier, the recipes have been adjusted so everything bakes at 400F. Due to the temperature and oven crowding things will take a little longer than you expect to cook. Don't panic. The entire board is Kosher, Halal, vegetarian (vegan if you substitute olive oil for the occasional use of butter) and everything but the rolls is gluten free. Feel free to flesh it out with some roasted turkey tenderloins from the Thanksgiving board to keep your meat eaters happy.

If you have leftovers, try chopping the mixed potatoes and onion into small pieces to make a breakfast frittata or home fries the next morning.

Hills = 8 cups roasted beets
Pasture = 8 cups herb roasted yellow potatoes
Forest = 8 cups honey roasted sweet potatoes
Mountains = 6 cups roasted purple potatoes
Fields = 6 cups herb roasted yellow carrots
Desert = 1 whole roasted onion
Bread = 12 whole wheat yeast rolls

Roasted Beet Hills

3 pounds red beets
3 tbsp olive oil
½ cup orange juice
2 tbsp raspberry balsamic vinegar
1 tbsp brown sugar
1 garlic clove, crushed
1 tsp table salt

Beets have an undeservedly bad reputation. I blame canned beets, which are, in fact, disgusting. So are canned asparagus and canned mushrooms. Don't be swayed by the worst possible iterations of any food. Real beets are surprisingly sweet and really tasty.

Start by peeling your beets. You probably want to put on an apron first, because handling beets will make you look like an extra in a zombie movie. Once your beets are peeled, cut them into quarter inch thick slices. Lightly coat the slices in olive oil and arrange them in a

single layer on a couple baking sheets. Bake the beets at 400F for 35-40 minutes. Use a spatula to turn them every 15 minutes.

While the beets cook, mix your raspberry balsamic vinegar, orange juice, brown sugar, salt, and thoroughly crushed garlic clove. Let the mix sit so the flavors will mingle.

As soon as you take the beets out of the oven, toss them in the orange juice mix. Let them sit in the glaze for 5 minutes before straining out any excess.

I opted for big round slices so the board wouldn't have such a monotonous texture, but you're welcome to cut your beets into ½ inch thick brick shapes if you prefer.

Honey Roasted Sweet Potato Forest

3 pounds sweet potatoes
8 tbsp (one stick) butter, melted
4 tbsp honey
1 tbsp cinnamon
2 tsp Kosher salt

I know these aren't green. Let me tell you, I wrestled over whether I should break with the roasted root vegetable theme and substitute in asparagus, broccoli, or even spinach. Fresh green veggies are expensive when out of season and this is most certainly a hearty fall board. In the end, I decided to break with the color scheme instead. You can think of these as sun bleached autumn logs if that helps.

Peel your sweet potatoes and cut them into nice, foresty logs. Arrange them in a single layer (or pretty close) in a large casserole dish.

Mix your melted butter, honey, cinnamon, and Kosher salt. Drizzle it on top of your sweet potato logs.

Bake at 400F for 50-60 minutes, or until the potatoes are tender.

Herb Roasted Yellow Potato Pasture

3 pounds yellow potatoes
¼ cup olive oil
1 tbsp basil
1 tbsp thyme
1 tbsp Kosher salt

Gently scrub your potatoes. You want to texturize the skin without peeling it off. Cut them into wedges and soak them in lightly salted water for 15 minutes. A lot of people swear by parboiling potatoes before roasting them, but I find this a ton easier.

While your potatoes are soaking, mix your olive oil, basil, thyme, and Kosher salt. (You now have 14 more minutes to kill, so you might as well start on some of the other root vegetables.)

When your potatoes are done soaking, drain them and dump them into the oil mix. Get all your potato wedges nice and greasy before spreading them in a single layer on a baking sheet. Try not to crowd them.

Bake the potato wedges at 400F for 40-45 minutes, turning once, or until nice and crispy.

Roasted Purple Potato Mountains

3 pounds purple potatoes
¼ cup olive oil
1 tbsp fresh ground black pepper
1 tbsp Kosher salt
1 tsp garlic powder
½ tsp onion powder

I know what you're thinking. Why use powdered onion and garlic when you could use the real things? The problem is, even if you throw garlic cloves and onions into a food processor and turn them into a paste, they don't make a good coating for crispy foods. On rare occasions, powders really are the best answer.

My grocery store carries baby purple potatoes. (You can also find them the size of small baking potatoes.) I like the baby variety because I can simply cut them in half.

Scrub the potatoes, cut them in half (or cube them if you have the larger variety) and toss them in lightly salted water. Do not put them in the same bowl with your soaking yellow potatoes. The purple color leaches slightly, so after 15 minutes you'll have somewhat smoky colored water. If you soak them together, your yellow potatoes will come out looking like they went bad a couple weeks ago.

While the potatoes soak, mix everything else in a large bowl. After 15 minutes of soaking, drain your potatoes, dump them in the olive oil mix, and get the spuds all lubed up and ready for the oven.

Spread them in a single layer on a baking sheet and roast the potatoes for 40-45 minutes, turning once, or until they're nice and crispy.

Herb Roasted Yellow Carrot Fields

3 pounds yellow carrots
¼ cup olive oil
2 tbsp Herbes de Provance
1 tbsp Kosher salt

Fun fact: carrots used to come in only yellow or red. The orange carrot we know today was a product of careful 17th century breeding to create a novelty carrot. The quirky orange ones were so popular they overtook both the previous colors.

Commercial orange, yellow and red carrots all taste pretty much the same (though the red ones will bleed into your food, making everything they're made with look like it should be fed to the zombies.) For our purposes, yellow carrots with flecks of green make nice fields.

Peel your carrots and cut them on the bias (which just means diagonally). Mix your olive oil, salt, and herbs in a big bowl. Smear the mix all over your carrots. Spread your oiled carrots in a single layer on a baking sheet.

Bake at 400F for 50-60 minutes. Pull them out at least twice to stir them up and respread the carrots or else you risk burning the bottoms.

Roasted Onion Desert

1 large white onion, peeled
2 tbsp olive oil
1 tsp Kosher salt

Drench your onion in olive oil. Sprinkle it with Kosher salt. Shove it onto the corner of a baking sheet holding either your carrots or potatoes. Let it bake for 35-40 minutes, turning every 15 minutes, or until the top turns a lovely caramel brown.

If you've never tried roasted onions before, the slices make amazing additions to warm sandwiches.

Browned Butter Whole Wheat Yeast Rolls

3 cups whole wheat flour
1 ½ cups warm water
1 tbsp yeast
4 tbsp butter
2 tbsp unsweetened cocoa powder
½ cup honey
1 tsp table salt

Start by browning your butter. This adds a wonderfully nutty flavor for next to no work. Plus, it sounds a lot more impressive than it really is.

Simply melt your butter in a skillet over medium high heat. It'll turn into a liquid, get frothy, get liquidy again, and eventually start to change color. You want to stir it pretty often. Once the butter starts to change color, keep an eye on it. There's very fine line between delicious caramel colored liquid and a black clot of horror. When in doubt, err on the side of not terribly brown. Take it off the heat and set it aside.

You want to do this before you start your yeast proofing so the butter will have time to cool down. If it's too hot when you mix everything up, it'll murder your yeast. You just brought that stuff out of suspended animation. Don't let the yeast die before it fulfills its purpose in life. (Namely, inflating your bread.)

While your browned butter cools, mix the yeast and warm water. Give it a good stir, then leave it alone for ten minutes while it blooms. When you come back, mix in the honey, cocoa powder and salt. After that becomes an undifferentiated slurry, mix in a cup of the whole wheat flour. Once that's well integrated, you can add your cooled browned butter. Give it another mix then add the rest of the flour.

If you have a stand mixer, attach the dough hook, set it to speed 2, and let it knead your dough for 5-6 minutes. If you're kneading by hand, keep it up for 6-10 minutes.

Cover the dough with a clean kitchen towel and let it rise for an hour.

When you come back, punch down the dough. Spread more whole wheat flour across a clean surface and roll the dough out into a large rectangle. Take a look at your hex shaped cookie cutters. You need at least 12 rolls to complete the board. Let that dictate how thin you roll the dough.

Butter a cookie sheet. Cut your dough into hexes and arrange them at least 3 inches apart. You don't want them to touch or else they'll end up misshapen. Let the rolls rise for another hour. If you want to pretty them up, whisk an egg with ½ tsp vanilla and 1 tbsp of water and use a pastry brush to paint the tops of the rolls. The vanilla isn't strictly necessary but it makes them smell amazing.

Bake the rolls at 350F for 15-18 minutes, or until they turn a lovely, dark golden brown.

Ports: trade garlic mashed potatoes for the roasted onion; trade the browned butter rolls for gluten free jalapeno cornbread from the Vegetarian Southern Map to make the entire board gluten-free

Home Made Chips and Dips Map

The brand Food Should Taste Good makes a line of hex shaped blue corn chips. I'm not saying the company is run by Settlers fans, but someone out there really wants you to have snackable oceans that line up with your board.

If you're pressed for time, you can always stop by your grocery store and pick up half a dozen refrigerated dips to fill out this board. Take a look at the recipes first. You may be shocked how easy it is to make your favorite dips. Save cash, add flavor, and impress your friends.

I used the small, ½ cup sized dishes for this board. All 19 hexes and a bunch of chips fit on a 15" pizza tray, making it easy to move the snacks around.

Hills = 1 ½ cups salsa
Forest = 2 cups guacamole
Pasture = 2 cups spinach dip
Mountains = 1 ½ cups black bean dip
Fields = 2 cups bar cheese
Desert = ½ cup ranch dressing
Ocean = blue corn chips

Basil Spinach Dip Pastures

¼ cup fresh basil leaves
4 cups fresh spinach leaves
2 tbsp olive oil
1 small onion, chopped
1 clove garlic, minced
1 cup cream cheese, softened
1 cup sour cream
Juice of ½ lemon
1 tsp Kosher salt
pinch red pepper flakes
3-4 drops green food coloring (very optional)

Stuff your basil, spinach, onion, garlic, and olive oil in a food processor and pulse until you have a slightly chunky liquid. Add the salt, red pepper flakes, lemon juice, and food coloring (if you really want to use it). Pulse a couple more times to mix it all in.

In a large bowl, mix your softened cream cheese and sour cream until they become a single dairy creation. Dump the contents of your food processor into the dairy and mix it all up until you have a thick green(ish) paste. My green came out a little more pastel than I intended. I think you're fine without it, but if you're (understandably) determined to keep up the color scheme, go ahead and add a full tsp of green food coloring.

Black Bean Dip Mountains

2 14-oz cans black beans, drained
1 cup salsa (use the recipe above)
2 cloves garlic
1 tbsp olive oil
1 tbsp chili powder
1 tsp smoked paprika
1 tsp cumin
1 tsp Kosher salt
Juice of 1 lime

Once more, put everything in your food processor and let it whir away until all the solids become a single, uniform paste. Let it sit for 4-6 hours (or overnight) for the best flavor.

Bar Cheese Fields

1 15-oz jar Cheese Whiz (or generic store brand)
¼ cup prepared horseradish
1 tsp Worcestershire sauce
½ tsp dry mustard powder
½ tsp garlic powder

Simply dump everything in a bowl and mix until it's well blended. Cover it with plastic and let it sit in the fridge overnight for the best flavor.

Ranch Desert

1 cup sour cream
½ tbsp white vinegar
1 tsp parsley
1 tsp dill
½ tsp garlic powder

½ tsp onion powder
½ tsp table salt

Mix the sour cream and vinegar until smooth. Add everything else and keep mixing until it's well blended.

That's it. Ranch dip is a lot easier than people think. Cover and refrigerate for at least 2-4 hours, or overnight.

Salsa Hills

Use the recipe from the Breakfast Taco Board

Guacamole Forest

In the name of efficiency, once more use the recipe from the Breakfast Taco Board.

Ports: substitute red bell pepper hummus from the Mediterranean Map for bar cheese
Robber: steal all the green food coloring

Deconstructed Paella Board

Traditional Spanish paella is made using about half the ocean's seafood plus a handful of spicy sausage to give it some kick. Here in the United States, where we vastly prefer our meat to be land based, Paella is most often made with a mix of chicken and sausage. The meat gets a lot of attention, but the real star of this dish is the saffron.

You can make this gluten free board two ways - entirely vegan or with a hearty mix of chicken and smoked sausage. To keep it as configurable as possible for a diverse group, I've made the base itself vegan with the meats as optional add-ons for individual hexes.

I used the ½ cup smaller dishes. That way, everyone can grab 3-4 hexes with their favorite toppings in order to customize their own paella.

Hills = red bell peppers
Forest = cilantro
Pasture = green peas
Mountains = smoked sausage or roasted garlic
Fields = turkey tenderloins or lemon wedges
Desert = chopped onions
Ocean = crusty bread

Paella Base

4 cups veggie broth
2 cups medium grain rice
2 tbsp olive oil
1 large pinch saffron threads
¼ cup warm water
2 red bell peppers, seeded and diced
1 ½ cups frozen green peas
1 ½ white onions, diced
4 cloves garlic, minced
½ tbsp Kosher salt
1 tsp sweet paprika
½ tsp turmeric

Lightly crush the saffron threads between your fingers before dropping them into a quarter cup of warm water. Set the soaking saffron aside.

Now grab your biggest skillet. I'm not kidding. It needs to be pretty huge. (You can also use a dutch oven.) Add your olive oil and bring the pan to a medium-high heat. Once it's nice and hot, toss in one diced onion. Let the onion cook until it turns translucent, stirring frequently. Now add the minced garlic and continue cooking until both the garlic and onion start to brown.

Sprinkle the onion and garlic mix with your sweet paprika, Kosher salt, and turmeric. Mix well and continue cooking the mix for another 2-3 minutes while it becomes seductively aromatic. Now add your rice. Stir pretty much continuously for the next 2 minutes. The rice should start to crackle as it toasts.

Drown everything in the veggie broth. While you're at it, throw in the saffron water. Mix it all thoroughly and wait for it to come to a boil.

Reduce the heat to medium low. I know you'll be tempted to mess with it, but leave the rice alone for 20 minutes while it cooks down. After 20 minutes, add 1 cup each frozen peas and 1 diced bell pepper. Stir once then step back and leave it alone. Let the rice mix cook for another 5-10 minutes, or until it's dry.

Omnivore Option

If you're making meat, follow the turkey tenderloin recipe in the Thanksgiving Board.

While you're shopping for turkey tenderloins, also pick up some summer sausage. They make this in low fat, all turkey, all beef, and an assortment of other varieties. Pick whichever one your crew will eat.

While the paella is cooking, heat a tablespoon of oil in another skillet over medium heat. Slice ½ pound of summer sausage into coins. Toss them in the olive oil and cook until they start to brown up and smell delicious.

Vegan Option

Roasted garlic is surprisingly easy. Simply cut the top off a head of garlic so the raw cloves are exposed. No need to peel it. Now drizzle it with olive oil and a pinch of salt and pepper. Wrap the clove in aluminum foil and bake it at 400F for 30-35 minutes. If you want to bake several heads, put them in a muffin tin so the collection is easier to fish out of the oven. Let the garlic cool for at least 15 minutes. You should be able to touch it with your bare hands. At that point, just squeeze and the soft, spreadable, caramel colored cloves will pop right out.

Assembly

You want to use the smaller disposable hex dishes for this board. Fill all 19 hexes with the rice mix until you're level with the lip, then make a little well in the center of each dish. In one, sprinkle your raw, chopped onion desert. Use your remaining bell pepper to create the hills.

Make forests from appropriately leafy cilantro and pasture from your remaining green peas. (Microwave them first so they're warm all the way through.) If you're serving carnivores, add mountains of smoked sausage and fields of turkey tenderloins. If you prefer the vegetarian option, substitute roasted garlic clove mountains and lemon wedges for fields.

Lemon wedges are traditional with paella (a fresh squeeze of lemon is especially nice with the seafood versions.) Even if you're serving the meat-tastic paella, keep a bowl of sliced lemons nearby.

Buy a loaf of crusty bread and cut it into a dozen slices to surround the board.

I like this deconstructed version of paella. For one thing, people either love or hate cilantro. Keeping it on distinct hexes makes everyone happy. For another, since everything is in distinct containers, you can still serve both vegetarians and meat eaters the same meal. The base is vegan, so each group can simply grab the hexes they prefer. Your guests can dump their selection of hexes on a plate, mix them together, and enjoy a custom paella.

If you know for certain you're not serving any vegetarians or vegans, the meat will be more flavorful if cooked in the sauce.

In that case, go ahead and dice up two chicken breasts. Cook those along with the summer sausage until they're nicely browned on the outside and cooked through. Reserve a handful of each meat for decorating the hexes and. Add the rest to the pan after toasting the rice and before adding the broth.

Indian Inspired Map

This is another delightfully obscure-diet-friendly map. Leave off the chapatis and the entire board is gluten free. Primal diners can chow down on chicken tikka masala, curried green beans, and cucumber salad. Vegetarians can enjoy a complete protein with the rice and beans plus a couple tasty veggie sides. Substitute the dal recipe for the chicken tikka masala and the whole board becomes Kosher, Halal and vegetarian.

Hills = 8 cups chicken tikka masala or dal
Forest = 6 cups curried green beans
Pasture = 6 cups cucumber salad
Mountains = 8 cups channa masala
Fields = 8 cups saffron rice
Desert = 2 cups raita
Ocean = 12 chapati

Chicken Tikka Masala Inspired Hills

4 boneless, skinless chicken breasts
1 cup plain yogurt
1 cup heavy cream
6 oz tomato paste
1 tbsp butter
juice of ½ lemon
4 tsp paprika, divided
4 tsp ground cumin, divided
2 tsp ground coriander, divided
2 tsp Kosher salt
1 tsp cinnamon
2 garlic cloves, minced
1 inch knob fresh ginger, minced
½ tsp cayenne pepper (more if you like it hot)

Cut the chicken breast pieces into strips. Remember, you'll be piling these into hills soon, so think in terms of stackability.

Mix the yogurt, lemon juice, 2 tsp paprika, 2 tsp cumin, and 2 tsp coriander in a large bowl. Add the chicken pieces and thoroughly coat them. Cover and refrigerate

for at least 4 hours. It's fine if you do this before work and come back to it when you get home 8-10 hours later.

Discard the marinade and very lightly rinse the chicken. If you have a grill, thread the pieces onto skewers and grill them until the juices run clear. If you don't, add 2 tbsp of olive oil to a large skillet and cook the chicken over medium-high heat until cooked through, about 8-10 minutes.

Meanwhile, melt the butter in another skillet over medium heat. Cook the minced garlic and ginger for 4-5 minutes so it becomes nice and aromatic. Add the remaining spices and cook for another 3-4 minutes. Don't skip this step. Cooking the spices brings out the flavor.

Add the tomato paste and stir until it absorbs all the spices. Next add the heavy whipping cream. Stir until well blended, then turn the heat down to low, cover, and simmer for 20 minutes while the flavors mingle and the sauce thickens. Add the chicken and simmer for another 5-10 minutes before serving.

Vegan Dal Hills

2 cups red lentils
6 cups veggie broth
2 tbsp olive oil
3 Roma tomatoes, chopped
3 cloves garlic, crushed
1 yellow onion, finely chopped
1 inch knob peeled ginger, minced

1 tbsp garam masala
1 tbsp turmeric
1 tsp Kosher salt
1 tsp red food coloring (optional)

Put a stockpot over medium heat. Add the olive oil, garlic, onion, and ginger. Mix it well then cook for 3-4 minutes, or until the garlic starts to brown. Add the garam masala, turmeric, and Kosher salt. Keep cooking for another 1-2 minutes to let the flavors mingle.

Now pour in the veggie broth and bring it to a boil. Add the lentils, tomatoes, and food coloring (if you're obsessed with color coordinating the board. Otherwise, the dal will be a light orange.)

Keep the heat at medium and let everything cook uncovered, stirring occasionally for 15-20 minutes, or until the lentils are soft and the volume is reduced by at least 1/3.

If you prefer your dal smooth, take it off the heat and let it cool slightly, then process it in a blender or food processor. I like mine with a little texture.

Channa Masala Mountains

2 15-oz cans of chickpeas, drained
¾ cup water
1 onion, diced
1large tomato, diced
2 garlic cloves, crushed
1 inch knob of garlic, peeled and minced
1 jalapeno, seeded and diced (optional)
2 tbsp olive oil
1 tbsp garam masala
1 tsp Kosher salt
1 tsp turmeric
1 tsp ground coriander
½ tsp ground cumin

Pour your olive oil into a large skillet. (If you're not worried about making this a vegan offering, try substituting ghee or butter.)

Cook the onions (and jalapeno, if you're using it) over medium-high heat for 4-5 minutes, or until they turn translucent. Add. the garlic and ginger. Keep cooking, stirring frequently, for another 3-4 minutes. Add the garam masala, turmeric, coriander, cumin, and salt. Give those a good stir and keep cooking for another 3-4 minutes to really bring out the flavor in the spices.

Finally, add your diced tomato, strained chickpeas, and water. Mix well, then turn the heat down to medium. Simmer for 15-20 minutes to really bring out the flavors.

Curried Green Bean Forest

1pound fresh green beans, ends trimmed
3 large tomatoes, diced
1 red onion, sliced thin
1 jalapeno pepper, seeded and sliced (optional)
2 garlic cloves, minced
1 inch knob ginger, peeled and minced
2 tbsp olive oil, ghee, or butter
1 tsp turmeric
1 tsp ground mustard seeds
1 tsp garam masala
1 tsp Kosher salt
½ cup water

Heat the oil in a large saucepan over medium heat. Add the sliced onions (and jalapeno, if you're using it) and cook for 3-4 minutes, until they're fully translucent. Now add the garlic, and ginger. Keep cooking for another 3-4 minutes, stirring occasionally. Add the turmeric, garam masala, salt, and ground mustard seeds (not the prepared mustard in your fridge. This is a totally different flavor). Keep cooking for another 3-4 minutes, stirring frequently.

Once the spices are nice and aromatic, add the diced tomatoes and fresh green beans. Stir until both are thoroughly coated. Add the water. Once it comes to a boil, slap a lid over that skillet and turn the heat down to medium.

Cook for 15-20 minutes, or until the beans are soft. Uncover and keep cooking for another 5-8 minutes while the sauce thickens.

Cucumber Salad Pasture

2 medium cucumbers
¼ cup rice wine vinegar
2 garlic cloves, crushed
½ inch knob ginger, peeled and minced
½ tsp Kosher salt
½ tsp fresh ground black pepper

Mix everything but the cucumbers in a large bowl. While the flavors are mingling, cut your cucumbers into thin rounds. Mix the cucumbers in the sauce until every piece is coated. Leave it in the fridge for an hour before serving.

Saffron Rice Fields

2 cups basmati rice
4 cups water
1 tbsp olive oil or ghee
½ tsp table salt
1 pinch saffron threads

Rice is one area where I believe strongly in taking shortcuts. I got my first rice cooker years ago and have never looked back.

Thoroughly rinse your rice in cold water. Strain out the water and rinse it a second time. (This really does make

a difference in the final texture.) Dump your rice, water, oil or ghee and table salt into a rice cooker and mix enthusiastically.

Gently sprinkle your saffron threads on top of the water. Don't mix them in. Just spread them out as much as possible and leave them alone.

Turn your rice cooker on and let the machine work its magic. When you come back, you'll have beautiful basmati rice with a top coat of saffron infused grains. If you really want to make it more aromatic, try bruising a cardamom pod and two whole cloves and adding those to the water mix. If you do, be careful to fish out the whole spices before serving.

Raita Desert

2 cups Greek style yogurt
1 cucumber
2 tbsp mint leaves
½ tsp sugar
½ tsp table salt
½ tsp ground cumin
pinch ground coriander

Peel and seed your cucumber. Mince the remainder.

Mix everything else in a large bowl. Add the cucumber pieces. Cover and refrigerate for at least one hour before serving.

Chapatis

2 cups whole wheat flour
1 cup water
1 tsp salt
non-stick cooking spray

These easy Indian flatbreads are similar to whole wheat tortillas.

Mix your flour, water, and salt until you have a sturdy dough. Knead it on a floured surface for a couple minutes. Turn your big ball of dough into 12 small balls of dough. Roll each one out as flat as possible. In an ideal world, they'll end up about the same size as the interior of your favorite skillet.

Put your skillet over a medium-high heat. Once it's nice and hot, spritz it with nonstick cooking spray and immediately throw in one of your freshly rolled out chapatis.

These cook super fast. Leave your chapati in there for 30 seconds then flip it. Leave the second side in there for 30 seconds then flip it again. If you're lucky, your chapati will start to balloon up into a ball. Use a clean kitchen towel to press it down flat, then remove it from the heat. If yours doesn't balloon up, just cook it for another 30 seconds before removing it from the heat.

Try not to shove the fresh, warm chapatis directly into your face. You need 12 of them to complete the board.

Ports: trade naan bread for chapatis; trade plain basmati rice for the saffron rice

Thanksgiving Dinner Board

This board is great for people hosting a holiday orphan Thanksgiving. Whether your guests are students enjoying their first American Thanksgiving or friends who can't make it home to their families, everybody gets to enjoy a traditional meal with turkey, dressing, corn, and pumpkin while also keeping it casual. Best of all, everything has been simplified so you can make an entire impressive Thanksgiving spread in just a few hours.

Hills = 8 cups basil roasted carrots
Forest = 8 cups garlic butter green beans
Pasture = 8 cups dressing
Mountains = 3 lbs turkey tenderloins
Fields = 6 cups sweet corn with garlic butter
Desert = 2 cups mashed potatoes and gravy
Ocean = 12 pumpkin stuffed sweet rolls

Basil Roasted Carrot Hills

4 pounds carrots
4 tbsp olive oil
4 tbsp basil
2 tsp Kosher salt

If you can find red carrots at your local health food store, schmancy food store, or farmers market, the bright color difference is worth a couple extra bucks. For the purpose of this board, nod and smile and pretend those bricks are more red than orange.

Peel your carrots and thinly slice them. Heat the olive oil in a large saucepan over medium heat. Add all of your carrots and stir until they're a little oily.

This is a slow food recipe. Let the carrots cook for about 35-40 minutes, stirring every five minutes. The edges will turn a dark brown as they caramelize. Don't try to rush it. The slow cooking does amazing things to the texture. When you're finished, they should be soft inside and slightly crisp on the outside.

Mix the basil and salt. Sprinkle the spice mix over your carrots, stirring well so they're all coated. Cook for another 5 minutes. Resist the temptation to add the herbs earlier. If you do, they'll burn, rendering your carrots inedible.

Garlic Butter Green Bean Forest

2 pounds fresh green beans
garlic butter sauce from the pasta board

Fill a stockpot with enough water to thoroughly drown your green beans. While that comes to a boil, snip the ends off your beans.

You probably still have some time to kill, so prepare an ice bath while you're waiting. Before the beans cook, you want to have a strainer waiting in one half of your sink and a large bowl of ice water in the other (or on the counter if you don't have a double sink.)

Once the water finally gets around to boiling, throw in your green beans. Let them cook for about 4 minutes to achieve the coveted tender-crisp texture. Immediately strain them then dump your steaming beans into the ice water. This stops the beans from cooking and preserves their color.

I'll be honest with you. Getting the green beans to stand up nicely in these hex dishes is a pain. If they're deliciously oily from garlic butter or other sauces, getting them to stand up is nearly impossible. If you're all about presentation, go ahead and arrange your beans dry with a discrete gravy boat of garlic butter hovering nearby. The garlic butter is also really good on the carrots and mashed potatoes. In fact, don't be surprised if it's as popular as your gravy.

Dressing Pastures

8 cups dried bread cubes
8 tbsp (one stick) butter or vegan butter substitute
6 cups chicken broth or veggie broth
2 onions, diced
2 stalks celery, diced
2 granny smith apples, peeled and diced (optional)
2 eggs, beaten
1 tbsp sage
1 tbsp Kosher salt
1 tsp basil
1 tsp thyme

Thanksgiving trivia time! The difference between stuffing and dressing is stuffing goes in the bird while dressing is made in its own container. Since we're simplifying things by making turkey tenderloins instead of a whole bird, this side dish is dressing.

Preheat your oven to 350F.

Melt 2 tbsp of butter in a large skillet over medium-high heat. Cook the onions, celery, and apples until the onions start to brown. (I like apples in my dressing. Not everyone agrees. Leave them out if you're not a fan. If, on the other hand, you really enjoy a little sweetness with your savory side dish, try also adding 1 cup of raisins to the bread cubes.)

Once the onions brown, melt the rest of your butter. (If you add all the butter at once, the onions will drown instead of brown.) Throw in the sage, salt, basil and thyme and mix them well.

Before we move on, let's talk about your bread cubes. Maybe you bought a bag from the grocery store. I've done it myself. But trust me when I say you'll be a lot happier if you use any artisan loaf. A garlic and onion loaf or a Tuscan Focaccia or really anything with some herbs and flavor in it is a better choice than a bag of bread cubes. Eat a slice or two, cut the rest into slices and leave them out to dry overnight. The next day, cut them up into smallish pieces then put them in your food processor to get a little finer texture. (That last part isn't required. If you like chunkier dressing just cut your bread into one inch cubes.) A lot of your flavor comes from the bread, so pick yours accordingly.

Pour your butter and broth into a large rectangular baking dish. Add the beaten eggs. Mix everything until it becomes one dubious liquid mass. Now add the bread crumbs. You want to get them as evenly moistened as possible. I find it's easiest to just reach in there with your hands and knead it.

Once you're done, pat everything down so you have a nice, even top. Cover with foil and bake at 350F for 30 minutes. Remove the foil and continue cooking for another 15-20 minutes or until the top is a nice, crisp golden brown.

Honey Butter Sweet Corn Fields

Use the recipe from the All American Meatloaf Map

Turkey Tenderloin Mountains

3 pounds turkey tenderloins
3 tbsp olive oil or melted butter
3 tsp Kosher salt
3 tsp fresh ground black pepper
3 tsp kitchen herbs

You're welcome to bake an entire turkey if you like. Most people I know only eat the white meat, so if I'm not making a dramatic presentation turkey, I like to really simplify things but just baking some tenderloins. Sure, tenderloins are less traditional, but keep in mind you're probably serving this in hex shaped plastic weigh boats you bought online. Sometimes you need new traditions.

Simply rub your turkey tenderloins down with either olive oil or melted butter. Now coat each one with ½ tsp each of salt and pepper. You're welcome to add other kitchen herbs if you'd like. I'm a big fan of basil and thyme on my turkey.

Line a baking sheet with aluminum foil. Space out your tenderloins so they're not touching. Bake your antisocial turkey at 400F for 30 minutes. Let it rest for another 10 minutes before slicing.

Garlic Mashed Potato Desert

3 pounds baking potatoes
1 cup heavy cream
¼ cup butter
3 garlic cloves, minced
1 tbsp salt
2 tsp fresh ground pepper

Start a big saucepot of water boiling. This takes time, so while you wait, peel and cube your potatoes. Once the water comes to a boil, throw them in and put on the lid. Let the potatoes cook for about 15 minutes.

While the potatoes merrily boil away, melt 1 tbsp of butter in a skillet over medium-high heat. Add your minced garlic cloves and cook until they barely start to brown. This is a simple way to add a lot of richness to the flavor.

When the garlic starts to brown, add the rest of your butter. Once it melts, add the salt and pepper mix well, and turn off the heat. If you like your garlic mashed potatoes super garlicy, double the number of cloves.

When your potatoes have cooked for 15 minutes, strain them. I dump mine right back in the same pot. Add the garlic butter mix and heavy cream, then pound away with a potato masher until you reach your favorite texture.

Easy Brown Gravy

1 cup chicken or veggie broth
¼ cup red wine
½ cup water, divided
2 tbsp butter
2 tbsp flour
½ tsp black pepper
½ tsp Kosher salt

Melt the butter in a saucepan over medium-high heat. Add the red wine, broth, water, salt and pepper. Turn the heat down to medium-low and simmer for at least 15 minutes so the harshness has burned out of the alcohol and you're just left with flavor.

Meanwhile, whisk the flour and remaining ¼ cup of water together until the mix is free from lumps. After 15 minutes of simmering, add the flour mix. Whisk enthusiastically to keep lumps from developing.

Cook for another 2-3 minutes then remove it from the heat. Let the mix thicken for at least 10 minutes before serving. Feel free to toss in a clove of minced garlic or a pinch of your favorite kitchen herbs if you want to make your gravy a little more exciting.

Pumpkin Stuffed Sweet Rolls

Dough:
4 - 4 ½ cups bread flour
1 tbsp yeast
1 ½ cups milk
½ cup sugar
2 eggs
2 tbsp softened butter
1 tsp salt

Filling:
½ cup canned pumpkin
1 tbsp cinnamon
1 tsp allspice
½ tsp nutmeg
¼ tsp table salt
½ cup brown sugar
½ cup melted butter

Glaze:
2 cups powdered sugar
¼ cup canned pumpkin
1 tsp cinnamon
4 tbsp water

This recipe is similar to the Blueberry Stuffed Sweet Rolls from the Cold Salad board, but instead of summer berries, it's stuffed with pumpkiny autumn goodness. If you understandably prefer a nice blue ocean around your board, substitute those rolls instead.

To make these, start by heating the milk until it's the temperature of a warm bath. Mix in the yeast. Let that bloom for 10 minutes. Add the sugar, salt, eggs and softened butter. Mix it all into a single frothy mess. Now mix in the flour.

If you have a stand mixer, attach the dough hook and let it do the hard labor for the next 6-7 minutes. If you're kneading by hand, show that dough who's boss for the next 8-10 minutes. Once you have achieved a well-kneaded dough, cover it with a clean kitchen towel and let it rise for an hour. When you come back, dust a clean surface with flour, punch down your dough, and roll it into a large rectangle.

To make the filling, melt your butter in a microwave safe bowl. While that's melting, mix your canned pumpkin with the brown sugar, cinnamon, nutmeg, allspice, and salt in another bowl. Paint the dough rectangle with melted butter. Spread the pumpkin mix over it, leaving a one inch border on all sides. Carefully roll the dough along the long side until you now have a long tube of sweet holiday temptation. You may notice the filling has pushed its way to the ends. It's a good thing you didn't spread it all the way to the edge or else you'd have a huge mess.

Cut the tube into 1 inch slices. Instead of a huge mess, you now have a moderate sized one. There's no getting around it. Some of the filling is destined to gloop out. Arrange your rolls 3 inches apart on well greased cookie sheets. Don't put them any closer. You want big round pumpkiny cinnamon rolls, not scrunched in square ones.

Cover the dough with a clean kitchen towel and let the rolls rise for another hour. Bake them at 350F for 20-25 minutes, or until the tops are a dark golden brown. While the rolls bake, mix up your glaze. Whisk the powdered sugar and water together until you have a smooth paste. Add the pumpkin and cinnamon. It's that easy. Let the rolls cool completely before glazing.

Ports: trade basil carrots for candied yams or pumpkin pie slices for the pumpkin rolls
Year of Plenty: add cranberry sauce and browned butter yeast rolls

Grilled Rosemary and Cherry Tomato Road

4 fresh rosemary stalks (wood)
16 cherry tomatoes (bricks)
1 tbsp basil infused olive oil
1 tsp Kosher salt
1 bamboo skewer

Well, howdy neighbor! I saw you eyeballing that field. It sure is pretty, so I decided to use all my extra wood and brick to build a road right around it. Sorry if that blocks you off from the route you were taking to a port. Don't be so mad. You have to admit this is the best smelling road you've ever traveled. It's not that hard to build your own.

Start by freezing your fresh rosemary stalks overnight. The next morning, working against the grain, simply push all the leaves off the stalks. You should now have a nubby, somewhat brittle looking twig. Go team wood! Use your bamboo skewer (or an awl if you're stocked up on ore) to poke holes through the center of each cherry tomato. Now thread the frozen rosemary stalk through three tomatoes to make a kabob.

Drizzle your tomatoes with basil infused olive oil and sprinkle the tops with Kosher salt. If you don't want to buy basil infused olive oil, just buy a bunch of basil and some cheap olive oil. Roll the basil leaves up in your hands like you're crumpling paper into a ball. (This bruises it, releasing the oils.) Rip up the leaves and stuff them in the olive oil. Walk away for a week or three (the longer the better.) When you come back, you'll have simple, cheap infused oil. While you're at it, you might as well make some rosemary infused oil from all the leftover leaves.

These road kabobs are great on a grill. If you keep the lid down for five minutes, everything inside will be infused with wonderful smelling rosemary smoke. Once they've cooked for five minutes, open the grill use tongs to carefully turn the tomatoes over. Let them get a little blackened on at least one side.

If it isn't grilling season or you live somewhere you're not allowed to cook over open fire, you can always broil these. Don't be afraid of your broiler. I know many of you think it's a fire demon who exists only to burn your hands and blacken your food, but I promise the broiler is merely a neglected weapon in your arsenal against bland food.

Arrange the kabobs on a grill pan. If you don't have one, just put them on a cookie sheet. Put your rack six inches from the broiler and slide in the pan. Keep a very close eye on these. Mine went from split skins to blackened tops in about 4 minutes, though your oven may take anywhere from 3-6. As soon as the tops darken, pull the kabobs out of the oven.

Either way, the tomatoes come out beautifully juicy and with a wonderful herby flavor. They're fantastic with lamb kabobs. If you're feeling fancy, pull the tomatoes off the stem, wrap each one in a fresh basil leaf, put it on a wedge of mozzarella, and skewer the three together with a toothpick.

Grilled Asparagus and Bell Pepper Road

1 pound thin asparagus stalks (wood)
2 bell peppers (bricks)
¼ cup olive oil
¼ cup raspberry balsamic vinegar
2 garlic cloves, crushed
1 tsp fresh rosemary leaves (½ tsp dried)
1 tsp Kosher salt
½ tsp fresh ground black pepper

Hey, remember when you stabbed those rosemary stalks through the innocent hearts of baby tomatoes? In addition to herb infused olive oil, here's something useful to do with all those leftover rosemary leaves.

Think of this as a tall, proud tree lined road leading from your settlement to the nearest port.

Mix the olive oil, raspberry balsamic vinegar, garlic cloves, salt, pepper, and rosemary in a large, resealable plastic bag.

Seed both your red bell peppers and cut them into strips. Throw the bell pepper strips and asparagus into the plastic bag. Squeeze out as much air as possible before sealing it up. Let it marinate for at least 30 minutes, turning it over every 15 so the marinade soaks in evenly.

Drain the marinade. (It's all vegan, so you can safely use it as a glaze on other foods if you'd like.) If you're grilling outdoors, lay the asparagus and peppers on a hot grill (though not over direct flame). Let them cook for 7-10 minutes, or until the asparagus is crisp-tender and all the veggies have tasty char lines on both sides. This also works surprisingly well on an indoor electric grill.

Feel free to leave out the bell peppers and substitute this for any other forest recipe calling for asparagus or green beans.

Cold Buckwheat Salad Road

6 oz buckwheat noodles (wood)
1 large red bell pepper (bricks)
2 green onions
½ inch knob ginger, peeled and minced
3 tbsp rice wine vinegar
2 tbsp brown sugar
1 tbsp soy sauce
1 tbsp olive oil
2 tsp sesame oil
1 tsp Sriracha (optional)

Gosh, this road is pretty dark and wet. Are you sure you want to keep building in this direction? It seems like robber bait to me with all that brick and wood mixed up together.

You've heard about those guys stealing manhole covers for the metal, right? If you keep coming towards my pasture, I have a bad feeling a robber might do something similar to your ore. I'm not threatening you, of course, but there are two other directions you could go.

If you insist on building in this direction you might as well commemorate your demise with an edible homage to your unfortunate road.

Start by boiling the noodles according to package directions.

While the noodles are boiling heat your olive oil in a saucepan over medium-high heat. Seed your red bell pepper and slice it into thin strips. Throw those in the oil and let them cook down while you slice up your green onions. Slice the white parts nice and thin and throw them in with the red bell pepper strips. Roughly chop the greens and set them aside.

Cook your bell peppers and onions for 3-4 minutes, stirring occasionally. Once the onions start to brown, add the minced ginger, rice wine vinegar, brown sugar, soy sauce, sesame oil, and Sriracha (if you like hot sauce.) Turn the heat down to medium-low and keep stirring for another 2 minutes.

By now, your buckwheat noodles should be ready. Drain them, rinse the noodles in cold water, and shake the strainer a little bit to get off as much water as possible. Add the buckwheat noodles directly to the skillet full of bell pepper sauce.

Give it a good, thorough mixing so the noodles are completely coated in sauce and the veggies are thoroughly incorporated. Each bite should have a little wood and a little brick.

Chill for at least two hours (or just leave it in the fridge overnight. Nothing bad will happen. That just gives the flavors more time to mingle.) Just before serving, sprinkle the green onions on top.

Tomato and Cucumber Tree Lined Road

2 cucumbers (wood)
4 tomatoes (bricks)
10 fresh basil leaves
1 tbsp balsamic vinegar
½ tbsp rice wine vinegar
½ tbsp olive oil
pinch sea salt
4 oz herbed goat cheese (optional)

You know what this forest needs? Modern highway development. You've got scenic, ore filled mountains nearby fading into rusty hills full of rich claybeds. I know this forest is close to your pastures, but I promise nothing but the most ecologically friendly development of its resources. After all, in another turn I'll have a whole settlement full of people here relying on this forest for their livelihood. I'm sure they'll take good care of it.

Now, if you want to make a tree lined road of your own over there, on the other side of the desert, it's actually pretty easy.

Start by cutting your cucumbers in half. Use a spoon to scoop out all the guts and seeds. Now slice the cucumbers into long strips and cut them in half. The goal here is to end up with long, green stalks of cucumber. Think of these as lovely moss covered trees.

Next simply dice your tomatoes until they look like little bricks after a long rainstorm. Take half your fresh basil leaves and rip them into small pieces. Mix them in with the tomatoes

Arrange the cucumbers and tomatoes so your plate looks like a moss covered forest alongside a brick road. Try to keep the diced basil leaves on bottom of the tomato mix.

I found it easiest to keep my forest growing tall and proud if I spread a log of herbed goat cheese behind it and propped the cucumbers upright against them.

Mix your balsamic vinegar, rice wine vinegar, olive oil, and a pinch of sea salt. Lightly drizzle that over your cheerful woodland scene.

Raspberry Roads

Wood:
2 cups whole wheat flour
1 cup all purpose flour
1 cup packed brown sugar
5 tbsp room temperature butter
1 tbsp orange juice
1 tsp orange zest
2 eggs
1 tsp vanilla extract
2 tsp baking powder

¼ tsp baking soda
¼ tsp table salt

Bricks:
1 cup raspberry jam

These port roads get so much traffic. It's not too hard to reinforce them with a brick core and a wooden superstructure just wide enough to fit a standard cart wheel base. Lock and load. Or, lock in and ensure your cart keeps going in the right direction no matter how much you've been drinking.

In fact, I was so happy with that little engineering achievement I had the kitchens whip up some cookies to honor the inventor. Now, you and I know these roads would be evens sturdier with some metal reinforcement from all that ore your fine mountain people produce, but we can talk about that later.

If you like my raspberry roads, they're not that hard to make.

Start by creaming the eggs, softened butter, vanilla, and brown sugar. Responsible people will sift the flours, baking powder, baking soda, and table salt together, but I have the feeling my cook is pretty lazy. I can't tell the difference, so go ahead and dump everything but the jam into your bowl and mix it up until you have a dark, woody dough.

Cover the dough with plastic and tuck it into your fridge for a couple hours while it hardens up. When you're ready to use it, roll the dough into a long rectangle. Cut away the jagged edges, knead them together, and roll them into another rectangle.

Cut your dough into long strips about 4 inches wide. Paint the middle of your dough with raspberry jam. You want to lay down a generous layer, but make sure you only cover 1/3 of the dough, smack in the middle.

Now carefully fold one side over the filling. Once it's in place, fold the second side over the first. You now have a long, rectangular tube.

Cut the tube into 3 inch long cookies.

Put them seam side down on a well greased cookie sheet and cook at 375F for 12-15 minutes, or until they turn a dark golden brown and fluff slightly.

Let them cool for 5-10 minutes before shoving the warm cookies into your face. These are great for building symbolic roads across maps of our fine continent.

BUILDING COSTS: SETTLEMENTS

Mozzarella Settlement Salad

6 fresh mozzarella balls (sheep)
2 Roma tomatoes (bricks)
6 fresh basil leaves (wood)
6 tsp toasted breadcrumbs (grain)

Welcome to my settlement! Before we discuss what you'd like for your ore, please enjoy this lovely appetizer made from sheep, bricks, wood, and grain. I hope this goodwill gesture encourages you to visit my ports early and often. Confidentially, Yellow will poison your sheep and piss in your grain. You're so much better off trading with a reputable dealer like myself.

If you can get ahold of a good sheep's milk mozzarella, this is the place to use it. Those cheeses can be prohibitively expensive and, depending on where you live, pretty hard to find, so, confidentially, don't worry about substituting in either buffalo or cow mozzarella.

Preheat your oven to 425F. Spread a thin layer of breadcrumbs on a cookie sheet. Toast them for 3-5 minutes, or until they turn golden brown. You can always skip this step, but toasting brings out a lot of flavor. You've probably noticed this phenomenon first thing in the morning, when you decided against shoving a plain slice of buttered bread into your mouth without first subjecting it to a heated transformation.

Once your breadcrumbs are nice and toasted, fetch either a small hex shaped cookie cutter or a knife and all your patience. Either way, cut the mozzarella balls into 2 inch thick wedges and then cut those wedges into hexes.

Slice your roma tomatoes into ½ inch rounds.

Assemble the appetizers by folding a fresh basil leaf in half, topping that with a tomato round, and stacking your cheese hex above it. Finish each one off with a light dusting of toasted breadcrumbs.

One Bite Settlement Snacks

1 Roma tomato, diced (bricks)
4 oz herbed goat cheese (sheep-ish)
12 whole grain crackers (grain)
12 smoked almonds (wood)

What's that? You think your ore miners might have rickets and could be in need of more sunlight and dairy? I can help with that. Before we discuss what you need for that ore, take a bite of this. There's plenty more where it came from.

These simple appetizers are incredibly easy for me to assemble from the verdant fields of assorted grains, lovely almond trees of my forest, juicy Roma tomatoes that grow on the sides of my hills, and smooth, spreadable artisan cheeses made by my hard working farmers. Their lives would be so much easier if there was a little more metal around here, but we can talk about that later.

To assemble these, merely smear a whole grain cracker with your favorite herbed goat cheese. Press a couple wedges of Roma tomato into the surface and top it off with a deliciously crunchy smoked almond.

You know, these one and two bite appetizers really make me crave a whole meal. Before we talk about your ore monopoly, let's move on to the next course.

Settlement Spinach Salad with Honeyed Apple Vinaigrette

¼ cup pepitas (wood)
2 small red apples, quartered and seeded (bricks)
2 balls fresh mozzarella, cut into hexes (sheep)
¼ cup small ground croutons (grain)
2 cups baby spinach leaves
¾ cup olive oil
¼ cup apple cider vinegar
¼ cup fresh apple juice
1 ½ tbsp honey
1 tbsp dijon mustard
½ tsp table salt

I hope you enjoyed the appetizer. Before we settle down to some real negotiations over that ore, our next course is a locavore salad made from locally grown and delicately seasoned pumpkin seeds, fresh made sheep's cheese, apples plucked from our forest groves, and finished with a hint of crutons ground from last night's delicious herb bread. It's dressed with honeyed vinaigrette from my very own apiary. I'm sure Yellow can't offer you anything like this. Mostly because my road blocked Yellow's access to wood.

If you'd like to make your own settlement salad, start with the simple vinaigrette. Merely mix the olive oil, apple cider vinegar, apple juice, honey, dijon mustard, and table salt in a large mason jar or random resealable container. I like the jars because you can take out your tensions by shaking them angrily whenever trade deals go south.

To assemble the salad, merely lay down a bed of spinach, pile two corners with fresh apple slices, the other two corners with generous mozzarella hexes, and heap a stack of spiced pepitas (pumpkin seeds) in the middle. I like to serve the dressing on the side so people can decide how dry or sloppy they like it.

Settlement Pasta.

12 leaves basil, torn (wood)
½ cup sundried tomatoes in oil (bricks)
6 oz linguine pasta (grain)
½ cup shredded mozzarella cheese (sheep)
2 cloves garlic, crushed
½ tsp sea salt
½ tsp fresh ground black pepper

I'm ready for a little something heartier. Did you know my people gather fresh ground peppercorns from our substantial forests? Just looking at bags of them makes me think longingly of mountains. The hearty peppercorns are like little black edible grains of ore, except of course you can't melt them down and smelt them. I know. I've tried. The chef prepared a simple dish of hearty carbs, the sort of stick-to-your-ribs food appreciated by exhausted miners.

To make it, start by simply boiling the pasta according to package directions. While you're waiting, roughly chop the sundried tomatoes. Take out a little more of life's frustration by ripping the basil leaves into small pieces. Mix the tomatoes with the torn basil, crushed garlic, sea salt, and my beloved fresh ground black pepper to make a simple dressing.

When the pasta has fully cooked, drain it and quickly rinse it in cold water. Toss it in the bowl with the sundried tomatoes and mix it until everything is well coated in flavorful oils. Before serving, top it off with shredded mozzarella cheese.

Settlement Pancakes

¼ cup slivered almonds (wood)
1 cup sliced strawberries (bricks)
1 cup all purpose flour (grain)
1 cup whole milk (sheep)
3 tbsp white sugar
2 tbsp room temperature butter
2 tsp baking powder
½ tsp salt
1 large egg
½ cup whipping cream
1 tbsp brown sugar
1 tsp vanilla

Hey, I'm glad you could stay the night. Our settlement has a couple of breakfast options for you.

These pancakes evoke the richness of our lands with their fluffy grain goodness topped by clouds of sweetened cream as white as a fresh shorn lamb, slivered almonds from our forests, and sliced strawberries as red as our bricks.

Making them is pretty easy. Mix the flour, baking powder, and salt in a large bowl. Add the white sugar, egg, and milk. Mix the whole mess until you have a lump-free batter.

Melt a teaspoon of butter in a large, nonstick skillet over medium heat. Pour in a quarter cup of batter and let it spread. When bubbles start to form on top, use a large spatula to flip the pancakes. Continue cooking for around 2 minutes. The bottom should be golden brown and the middle should be dry and cooked through. Repeat until you run out of batter.

While the pancakes are cooking, add the whipping cream, brown sugar, and vanilla to a stand mixer and attach the wire whisk. Let that work its magic until your liquid has magically transformed into a cloud-like solid mass of whipped cream. If you don't have a stand mixer, you can achieve the same effect with a hand mixer and some patience.

Serve your fresh pancakes topped with strawberry slices, fresh whipped cream, and almond slivers.

Settlement Omelet

¼ red bell pepper, diced (bricks)
¼ cup sliced mushrooms (wood)
¼ cup yellow corn meal (grain)
¼ cup sheep mozzarella (sheep)
1 green onion
2 eggs
2 tbsp milk
2 tsp butter
pinch each salt and pepper

Nothing displays the richness of our land more than a hearty breakfast chock full of bell pepper bricks, mushrooms gathered from our woods, fresh mozzarella cheese squeezed from a fat and docile sheep, plus a dusting of cornmeal to give it a sweet crunch. I hear your miners are starting to mix their own blood with rocks and try to pass the result off as bricks. Really, I can help with that. Let's work together.

It's been so long since your people have had access to any seasonings for their morning eggs. Let me walk you through the process for making a proper omelet.

Bring a medium sized skillet up to a medium heat. Melt one teaspoon of your butter. Add the diced bell pepper, sliced mushrooms, and sliced white ends of your green onion.

Sautee those for 4-5 minutes or until the onions start to turn golden brown. Slide all that onto a plate and add the remaining teaspoon of butter to the now empty skillet.

While the butter melts, beat the eggs, milk, and salt and pepper into a frothy yellow mix as gold as my lush cornfields. Pour the mix into the skillet. Resist any temptation to touch it. Seriously. Leave the eggs alone. It's important that you use a boring medium heat. If the heat is too high, you'll cook the edges while the middle stays entirely liquid. Be patient.

When the egg has completely set but is still pretty liquidy, go ahead and add the veggie mix to one half. Top that with thin slices of mozzarella. Let the eggs continue to set for about another minute then oh-so-carefully use your largest spatula to fold the untainted side of the omelet on top of the veggie filled side.

If you ripped it or had an otherwise awkward time, make sure to flip the omelet over before serving so all anyone sees is the neat, orderly bottom. For all they know the whole thing looked like that before they cut into it.

Settlement Oatmeal

¼ cup raspberries (bricks)
¾ cup whole milk (sheep)
2 tbsp brown sugar (wood)
1 cup steel cut oats (grain)
3 ½ cups water
½ tsp vanilla extract
¼ tsp table salt

Y'know, I've heard over in Red the workers have plenty of grain but no wood or bricks. That must make for some bland mornings. Let me show you how we make oatmeal in our fine, well endowed settlement.

Bring the water to a boil in a medium saucepan. Add the steel cut oats and salt. Keep the oats boiling over medium heat for 25-30 minutes, or until deliciously tender.

Add the milk, vanilla, and table salt. Give it a good stir and keep cooking for another 10 minutes, checking in to stir occasionally.

Once the oats reach your desired thickness, ladle them into a bowl. Top with the brown sugar and raspberries, plus add a splash more milk for color.

City Pasta

½ lb spaghetti (grain)
½ lb buckwheat noodles (grain)
1 cup figs, halved and stemmed (ore)
1 medium yellow onion, sliced (ore)
4 garlic cloves, sliced (ore)
¼ cup olive oil

¼ cup balsamic vinegar
¼ cup water (or broth)
1 tbsp Herbes de Provance
1 tsp Kosher salt
1 tsp brown sugar

Listen, you don't understand. My settlers need that ore. It's been so long since they've seen any that they've entirely forgotten what it looks like. When I told them to make a pasta dish in homage to your great cities, they topped the two grains with figs, which kind of look like they're filled with rocks, plus onions and garlic, because, and I'm quoting here, "We dug 'em up outta the ground, so they's like rocks, ni?" I don't even know what "ni" means in that context. I could go to a library and look it up if we had the ore needed to build an actual city.

At least the food here is good. The key to this dish is all in the allegedly ore-like sauce. All you need to do to the pasta itself is boil it according to the package directions, mix it up so the colors are intertwined, and set it aside.

Meanwhile, put a large skillet over a medium-high heat. Add your olive oil and sliced onions. Stir them in pretty well and let those cook for 3-4 minutes, or until they turn translucent. Add the salt, sugar, herbs, water and vinegar and mix it all until well blended. Once you have a uniform mix, add the sliced garlic and all but a couple of the figs (set a few aside for garnishing). Keep stirring frequently while the sauce cooks for another 4-5 minutes.

To serve, pile a heap of noodles in the middle of a plate and top them with ¼ of the sauce. It's fairly sticky stuff, and a little goes a long way. Let your diners mix it in themselves while eating.

Moroccan Inspired City Lamb

¼ cup dried apricots, diced (ore)
¼ cup raisins (ore)
¼ cup golden raisins (ore)
4 cups cooked rice (grain)
2 Greek style pita breads (grain)
1 lb ground lamb (or beef)
2 tbsp tomato paste
1 tbsp turmeric
1 tbsp coriander

½ tbsp cumin
½ tbsp cinnamon
½ tbsp Kosher salt
½ inch knob fresh ginger, grated
1 tbsp olive oil
Juice of 1 lemon
½ cup boiling water
½ cup chicken or veggie broth

There they go again. My poor Settlers pretty much confuse any hard thing that will break their teeth with ore.

This time, in homage to your fine mountainous mines, the chef decided hard, dried fruit was close enough to ore. I need your help. I can't even threaten to throw rocks at their heads because they'd just confuse them with more ore and try to melt them down into metal. At least, that's what they tell me every time they set a rock on fire and toss it through my window.

To make this mountainous homage of food, start by boiling half a cup of water and adding all your ores. The raisins, golden raisins, and finely diced apricots need to rehydrate or else they really will feel like rocks in your mouth.

While the rocks soak back into fruit, add your olive oil to a large skillet over medium heat. Toss in the turmeric, coriander, cumin, cinnamon, salt, and ginger. Gently fry the spices for 3-4 minutes so they become wonderfully aromatic. Mix in the tomato paste. Now sprinkle on your ground lamb. The goal here is to thoroughly mix the lamb with the spices. Turn the heat up to medium-high and cook until the lamb is browned all the way through.

Add your broth and fruit, including the soaking water. Mix it in so the fruit is well incorporated with the lamb. Put a lid on it, turn the heat down to medium-low, and let the lamb simmer for the next 20 minutes so the flavors can mingle. Stir every 5 minutes or so. Take off the lid, give it another good stir, and turn the heat back up to medium. Let it keep cooking until most of the excess moisture is gone.

Complete the city homage by serving your ore infused lamb on a bed of hot basmati rice with a thick loaf of toasted Greek style pita.

City Pot Pies

Crust:
1 ¼ cups flour (grain)
¼ cup fine ground yellow cornmeal (grain)
8 tbsp cold butter
1 tsp salt
½ tsp fresh ground black pepper
4 tbsp cold water

Filling:
1 cup frozen green peas (ore)
1 cup corn kernels (ore)
1 cup diced carrots (ore)
1 cup diced onions
1 cup cooked, shredded chicken, packed
2 cloves garlic, minced
3 ½ cups full fat chicken broth
2 tbsp cornstarch
1 tbsp butter or olive oil
1 tbsp thyme
½ tbsp basil
½ tbsp oregano
½ tsp fresh ground black pepper

My people can't thank you enough for the ore. I know that flock of sheep I sent home with your envoys will be thrilled to meet your hungry miners. In celebration of this fine opportunity to expand our meager settlement into a respectable city, I humbly present these individual pot pies. Sure, the ores inside are actually made of once frozen vegetables, but my people are still adapting to the idea that ore means metal instead of any rock-like item.

These are an impressive first course when negotiating with nearby land holders. Making your own is both faster and easier than it looks.

Start by making the crust. Mix the salt, pepper, flour, and yellow cornmeal. Cut the butter into small cubes and drop them into the dry ingredients. Use your fingers to mash the butter into the flour blend until it turns into a crumbly solid.

Add the cold water to make those crumbles stick together. It'll still feel like it's going to fall apart any second. As long as it sticks together, that's okay. If it won't stick together at all, add another ½ tbsp of water. Pack the whole mess into a ball, wrap it in plastic, and put it in the fridge for at least an hour.

Meanwhile, make your filling. Don't be intimidated by the number of ingredients. This is actually really easy to assemble.

Melt your butter or olive oil in a stockpot. Add the garlic and onions. Cook those over a medium-high heat until the onions are translucent and the minced garlic starts to brown. Add in the diced carrots. (These should be about the same size as your corn and peas. That way, they'll cook at about the same speed.) Keep stirring for another minute or two.

Dump 3 cups of your full fat, full salt broth into a stockpot. Add the thyme, basil, oregano, and fresh ground pepper. Bring the whole mess to a boil. Add in your chicken, corn, and peas. Reduce the heat to a simmer and let it cook for another 10 minutes while the flavors mingle.

Mix your remaining ½ cup of broth with the cornstarch. Take a whisk to it and really beat out all the lumps. Pour the mix into your stockpot, stirring frequently. This is what thickens up your sauce and adds a nice creamy mouthfeel without needing any dairy. Continue to cook for another 2-3 minutes, then remove it from the heat and let it cool and thicken.

While the filling cools, preheat an oven to 375F. Grab your pie crust out of the fridge. Use your hands to press it pretty flat, then grab a rolling pin and roll it out to ¼ inch thickness.

Fetch either your hex shaped cookie cutter or a knife and all your patience, because it's time to make 8 big circles and 8 medium hexes.

Spray the interior of a muffin tin with nonstick spray. Gently press the circles of dough into each one. Use a fork to poke a couple holes in the bottoms. Bake them for 10 minutes.

When the bottom crusts come out of the oven, fill each one most of the way to the top with pot pie filling.

Carefully lay a hex top crust on each one. Don't worry about pressing it down. These will magically meld with the bottom crusts while baking. All you'll do now is weirdly deform them. If you didn't cut a hex shape out of the middle, cut a couple of venting slits in the top of each crust.

Bake the pot pies for 12-15 minutes, or until the top crusts are golden brown.

City Cookies

2 cups all purpose flour (grain)
½ cup almond flour (grain)
1 cup dark chocolate chips (ore)
1 cup peanut butter chips (ore)
1 cup crushed Heath toffee chips (ore)
1 cup (2 sticks) butter
¾ cup packed brown sugar
¾ cup granulated sugar
1 tsp vanilla extract
1 tsp baking soda
1 tsp salt
2 eggs

Nothing shows off the bounty of my new city's holdings like these lush, decadent cookies. Sure, we enjoyed plain old Chocolate Chip back in our settlement days, and yes, there was that horrible marketplace controversy over sweetened sheep dung being substituted for chocolate chips, but now that we're a city, we have health inspectors. Any rumors to the contrary are probably coming from Yellow.

We've added almond flour for extra protein, plus a hearty mix of dark chocolate chips, peanut butter chips, and toffee chips to symbolize the ores that let us build our sturdy city walls. These cookies are perfect for symbolically celebrating both the fertility of your fields and the richness of your ore veins.

Start by mixing your all-purpose flour, almond flour, salt, and baking soda in a bowl. This may seem pointless, but if you don't, you might end up with one one cookie that's all almond or another that doesn't rise at all due to a lack of baking soda. It's worth the extra 30 seconds of effort to homogenize everything.

In another bowl, cream your eggs, vanilla, butter, and sugars. Once those are a soupy mass, add the dry

ingredients and all three of your ores. Keep mixing until you have achieved a seductively sugary dough. Try not to cram too much of it in your face before baking.

Butter a baking sheet. Don't waste your nonstick cooking spray. This isn't health food.

Use your hands to roll the dough into golfball sized cookies and place them about 3inches apart.

Bake at 350F for 12-15 minutes, or until the cookies are golden brown.

City Pesto and Roasted Garlic Spiral Buns

2 ½ cups bread flour (grain)
½ cup yellow cornmeal (grain)
½ cup sundried tomatoes packed in oil (ore)
½ cup basil pesto (ore)
10 garlic cloves, minced (ore)

1 cup warm water
1 tbsp yeast
2 tbsp olive oil
2 tbsp sugar
1 tsp Kosher salt

In honor of the gemstones mined alongside your ores, my cook put together these dinner rolls stuffed with tomatoes like rubies, pesto like emeralds, and garlic like diamonds. He doesn't get out much.

To make your own, start by dissolving the yeast and sugar in a cup of warm water. Let that froth away and get bubbly for 10 minutes. Meanwhile, fish your sundried tomatoes out of their oil and mince them up. Dump them right back in the oil they came in, but this time add the garlic cloves and basil pesto to keep the tomatoes company. Mix it all up until you have a thick ore paste.

Once your yeast is nice and frothy, add the olive oil and Kosher salt. Mix that up then add your two grains. The yellow cornmeal gives the rolls a nice sweetness and a hint of texture. Attach a dough hook to your stand mixer and let that knead away for around 6 minutes. If you haven't used any of your precious ore to make a stand mixer, make one of the kitchen serfs knead it for about 10 minutes. Cover the dough and let it rise for about an hour.

When you come back, punch the dough down. Spread a little extra cornmeal on a clean surface and roll that dough out into a big rectangle. Spread the interior of the rectangle with an even layer of your ore paste, leaving a full inch clean on all the outermost edges.

Now roll up your dough like you're making savory cinnamon rolls. Cut the rolls two inches thick and put them cut-side-up in a muffin tin. Cover them once more and let the rolls rise for another hour.

When you come back, bake them at 350F for 12-15 minutes, or until golden brown.

Gem Stuffed City Pie

Crust:
2 cups all purpose flour (grain)
½ cup almond flour (grain)
1 cup cold butter
1 tbsp sugar
1 tsp salt
6-8 tbsp ice water

Filling:
1 cup frozen cherries (ore)
1 cup frozen raspberries (ore)
1 cup frozen blueberries (ore)
1 cup granulated sugar
4 tbsp cornstarch
¼ cup orange juice

I know you'll be heading home soon, but I wanted to wrap up our negotiations with a dessert so you'll remember us sweetly when you head back to your own cities. The same chef who thought he was being clever with the ore stuffed pesto rolls informed me he filled this pie with symbolic rubies, garnets, and sapphires as thanks for the hard work of your miners. I'm tempted to send him home with you so he can see what a real mine is like. He also fortified the crust with sugar and almond flour to give it an extra nutty sweetness.

To make the sweet crust, start by mixing the all purpose flour, almond flour, sugar and salt in a large bowl. Cut the butter into cubes and drop them into the flour mix. Use your fingers to work the butter into the flours until you achieve a coarse meal. Transform that meal into a dough by adding just enough water to make it all stick together. When in doubt, err on the side of less water.

Once it all sticks together, roll the dough into two equal sized balls, wrap them in plastic, and put them in the fridge for at least an hour.

Meanwhile, make your filling. Add all your frozen berry ores to a saucepan. Bring it to a medium heat and cover. Within 5-6 minutes, your berries should be swimming in their own juices. This is good.

Whisk your cornstarch into your orange juice until it's completely free of lumps. Add that to the berries along with your cup of sugar. From this point on, you are a stirring machine. Keep everything in motion until the sugar is completely melted and the cornstarch mix is completely integrated with the berries. Luckily, this should only take 2-3 minutes.

Remove the filling from the heat. While it cools, fetch your pie crusts from the fridge. One at a time, press each one flat with your hands then use a rolling pin to flatten it out until it fits in a 9 inch pie pan. Spread out the bottom crust and pop it into a 350F oven for 10 minutes to firm up.

Pull the crust out of the oven and fill it with your berry blend. Carefully top that with your remaining crust and pinch, flute, or otherwise seal the edges shut. If you're clever, you'll make a hex shaped vent hole in the middle. If not, just cut some slits in it with a knife.

Evenly sprinkle the top with another 2 tbsp of granulated sugar to give it a nice, sweet crunch. Wrap some foil or a pie protector around the outer crust.

Bake at 375F for 30 minutes. Remove the foil or pie protector and keep baking for another 20 minutes (50 total) or until the crust is entirely golden brown.

BUILDING COSTS: DEVELOPMENT CARDS

Lamb and Barley Development Card Stew

1 lb lamb stew meat (sheep)
1 cup pearled barley (grain)
1 tbsp Kosher salt (ore)
1 tbsp olive oil
1 yellow onion, peeled and chopped
2 large carrots, peeled and chopped
3 garlic cloves, minced

4 cups beef broth
1 tsp fresh ground black pepper
1 tsp thyme
1 tsp oregano
1 bay leaf

You know, now that we have roads leading to our ports and settlements that have grown into strong cities, I feel like my people need someone to properly protect them. In order to recruit good knights, you need to offer them good food. This hearty, winter stew will keep them fit and full during winter training with its big chunks of lamb, whole grains, and freshly mined salt. If you're not building an army, a bowl of this before dark will keep your lawkeepers well fueled for a night patrolling roads for robbers.

To nourish your own future knights, start by putting a stockpot over a medium heat. Add the olive oil and lamb. Let the lamb brown for 3-4 minutes on a side, then turn it and repeat the process. When the lamb is nice and browned, use a slotted spoon to fish it out of the stockpot. (You want to leave any nice juices in place.)

Add the onion and garlic and let them cook until the onion starts to brown. Now pour in the beef broth and give it a good stir. While you're at it, put everything but the barley in the pot.

Bring it all to a boil. Cover the pot, reduce the heat to medium-low, and let it all simmer for about an hour. This helps the flavors mingle while also breaking down a tough cut of meat.

After an hour, add your barley and give it all another good stir. Cover the pot and let it simmer for 45-60 minutes, or until the barley has completely absorbed most of the fluid and is nice and chewy.

Serve this hearty winter stew with some City Spiral Buns.

Lamb Kabobs Served on Pita

2 pounds boneless lamb leg, cut into large cubes (sheep)
1 12-oz bottle beer (grain)
2 tbsp brown sugar (ore)
2 cloves garlic, minced

1 tbsp olive oil
1 tsp paprika
1 tsp Kosher salt
1 tsp fresh ground black pepper

I dined recently at the governor's house. He said he liked to keep his food simple enough he wouldn't forget where he came from, yet developed enough everyone would realize he deserved to be in office despite his sudden and rather unexpected ascension.

According to him, beer marinades are the secret to developing great flavor while tenderizing tough cuts of lamb.

Start by mixing a bottle of whatever beer you normally drink, some rock-like brown sugar, minced garlic, olive oil, salt, pepper, and paprika in a large bowl. If you didn't buy precut stew meat, hack your lamb into large, 2-inch kabob sized squares and dump them in the marinade. Make sure all your meat chunks are well covered before refrigerating them for at least 2 hours. I like to let mine sit overnight.

Whenever you come back to the meat, thread it onto the skewers of your choice. Grill over hot coals no more than 6 inches above the heat source. If you really do grill them close to the heat, they should be done in no more than 5-7 minutes per side. If you leave them a foot or two up higher, you'll essentially be smoking the kabobs.

If it's not grilling season or you live somewhere you're not allowed to play with fire, arrange the kabobs on a meat rack (or anything that keeps the meat from touching the bottom of the pan) and broil them for 3-5 minutes per side, depending on your preferred doneness.

Serve on warm, fresh grilled pita with a skewer of Rosemary Stalk Roads

Lamb, Rice, and Fig Pilaf

1 cup fully cooked, shredded lamb (sheep)
2 cups long grain rice (grain)
1 ½ cups black mission figs (ore)
2 tbsp olive oil
1 small yellow onion, diced
3 cups beef or veggie broth
2 tbsp tomato paste
1 tbsp Kosher salt
2 tsp cinnamon
1 tsp coriander
½ tsp allspice

One of the best things about all this development has to be our new library. I wasn't sure what to do with all the new resources at the market. Cinnamon? Coriander? They look suspiciously like wood and ore if you ask me, but according to this book, they're apparently used in food.

Start by heating the oil in a large skillet over medium-high heat. Add the diced onion and cook for 3-5 minutes, or until it just starts to brown. Add the broth, then dump in the tomato paste, cinnamon, coriander, Kosher salt, and allspice. Whisk everything together until you have a lump-free, fragrant liquid.

As soon as the broth mix comes to a boil, add the rice and shredded lamb. (Leftover kabob meat works well for this. If you prefer, you can also buy ground lamb and simply brown it in a skillet before cooking the pilaf.)

Cover, reduce the heat to a simmer, and let it cook for 30 minutes. While you wait, cut the stems off your black mission figs and cut them in half. See, they really do look like something you'd mine.

After half an hour, the rice should be cooked through and the pan should be free from excess liquid. If there's still liquid, put the lid back on and let it cook for another 3-5 minutes.

Once you have achieved dry, fully cooked rice, fluff it with a fork while gently mixing in your fig halves.

Serve hot with warm pita bread.

Panko Breaded Meatballs

1 pound ground lamb, not lean (sheep)
2 cups panko breadcrumbs, divided (grain)
½ tbsp coarse ground black pepper (ore)
6 cloves garlic, minced
1 tbsp parsley
½ tbsp basil
1 tsp Kosher salt
2 large eggs

Remember when we were kids. The place wasn't so crowded, and it took everybody pitching in together just to scrape together enough wood and brick to make a road from the settlement to a port. We'd eat our meat on a stick and be happy to have a crust of bread to go with it, but no, these days, we're "developed." Kids don't want some tough old kabobs anymore. They want their meat ground up nice and soft, stuffed with spices and rolled in a crunchy coating.

If you've got your own "developed" generation of kids coming home from the university, you'd best serve them something they'll be familiar with from school. At least these are pretty easy to mix up.

Start by preheating your oven to 400F.

While it gets nice and hot, mix 1 cup of breadcrumbs with the salt, pepper, garlic, parsley, and basil. Add the ground lamb and both eggs. Knead everything together until you achieve a somewhat wet dough.

Form the meat dough into golfball sized meatball. Sop up that wetness by rolling your meatballs in the remaining breadcrumbs.

Don't give into the temptation to make oversized meatballs. Anything bigger than a golfball will still be pink inside when the outside is a dark, crispy brown. Bigger meatballs will either end up dangerously rare or unpleasantly burned.

Line up your meatballs on a baking sheet. They will leak a little grease (which is delicious sopped up with bread) so make sure your baking sheet has a lip on it.

Bake the meatballs for 30 minutes. They should come out tender inside and crispy outside. They're great both hot and fresh out of the oven or stuffed into a cold sandwich the next day.

Appendix

GLUTEN ALLERGIC OR CELIAC DISEASE - 63 recipes

All American Meatloaf Map - pg 30
- Clove and Honey Pea Pastures
- Garlic Butter Asparagus Forest
- Sweet Corn Fields

Barbecue Board - pg 42
- Coleslaw Pasture
- Potato Salad Fields
- Pulled Chicken Barbecue Hills

Breakfast Taco Map - pg 21
- Guacamole Pastures
- Salsafied Hills
- Sausage-ish Mountains

Deconstructed Paella Board - pg 60
- Everything but the bread garnish

Deconstructed Salad Nicoise - pg 33
- Entire Board

Fish Fry Board - pg 35
- Broccoli Slaw Pastures
- Garlic and Lemon Red Skinned Potatoes Hills and Green Beans Forests
- Tartar Sauce Desert

Home Made Chips and Dips Map - pg 57
- Basil Spinach Dip Pastures
- Black Bean Dip Mountains
- Ranch Desert

Indian Inspired Map - pg 63
- Chicken Tikka Masala Inspired Hills
- Chana Masala Mountains
- Cucumber Salad Pasture
- Curried Green Bean Forest
- Raita Desert
- Saffron Rice Fields
- Vegan Dal Hills

Mediterranean Map - pg 27
- Cucumber Salad Forest
- Keema Pastures

- Roasted Red Bell Pepper Hummus Hills
- Tzaziki Desert

Pasta Board - pg 49
- Alfredo Desert
- Basil Marinara Hills
- Garlic Butter Fields
- Pesto Pastures

Roasted Root Vegetable Board - pg 52
- Herb Roasted Yellow Carrot Fields
- Herb Roasted Yellow Potato Pasture
- Honey Roasted Sweet Potato Forest
- Roasted Beet Hills
- Roasted Onion Desert
- Roasted Purple Potato Mountains

Settlers of the Cold Salad - pg 11
- Brown Lentil Mountains
- Cantaloupe, Banana and Pineapple Salad
- Cold Cucumber Salad Desert
- Green Bean Salad Forest
- Green Goddess Grape and Melon Pasture
- Raspberry Balsamic Watermelon Hills

Settlers of the Nacho Bar - pg 24
 - Entire Meal

Thanksgiving Dinner Board - pg 68
- Basil Roasted Carrot Hills
- Garlic Butter Green Bean Forest
- Garlic Mashed Potato Desert
- Turkey Tenderloin Mountains

Vegetarian Southern Map - pg 45
- Gluten Free Fried Okra Pastures
- Pork Free Collard Green Forests
- Sweet Gluten Free Jalapeno Cornbread
- Southern Fried Apple Fields
- Vegetarian Red Beans and Rice Hills

Waffle Bar Map - pg 15
- Bananas Foster Fields
- Whipped Cream Desert

Building Costs
- Grilled Rosemary and Cherry Tomato Road - pg 72
- Grilled Asparagus and Bell Pepper Road - pg 73
- Lamb, Rice and Fig Pilaf - pg 93
- Moroccan Inspired City Lamb (without pita) - pg 85
- Mozzarella Settlement Salad (without breadcrumbs) - pg 78
- Settlement Spinach Salad with Honeyed Apple Vinaigrette (without croutons) - pg 80
- Tomato and Cucumber Tree Lined Road - pg 75

LACTOSE INTOLERANT AND MILK ALLERGIC - 50 recipes

All American Meatloaf Map - pg 30
- Clove and Honey Pea Pastures

Barbecue Board - pg 42
- Coleslaw Pasture
- Potato Salad Fields
- Pulled Chicken Barbecue Hills

Breakfast Taco Map - pg 21
- Guacamole Pastures
- Salsafied Hills
- Sausage-ish Mountains

Deconstructed Paella Board - pg 60
- Entire Board

Deconstructed Salad Nicoise - pg 33
- Entire Board

Fish Fry Board - pg 35
- Broccoli Slaw Pastures
- Mountains of Beer Battered Fried Fish

Home Made Chips and Dips Map - pg 57
- Black Bean Dip Mountains

Indian Inspired Map - pg 63
- Chana Masala Mountains
- Chapatis
- Cucumber Salad Pasture
- Curried Green Bean Forest
- Saffron Rice Fields
- Vegan Dal Hills

Mediterranean Map - pg 27
- Cucumber Salad Forest
- Roasted Red Bell Pepper Hummus Hills

Pasta Board - pg 49
- Basil Marinara Hills

Roasted Root Vegetable Board - pg 52
- Herb Roasted Yellow Carrot Fields
- Herb Roasted Yellow Potato Pasture
- Honey Roasted Sweet Potato Forest
- Roasted Beet Hills
- Roasted Onion Desert
- Roasted Purple Potato Mountains

Settlers of the Cold Salad - pg 11
- Brown Lentil Mountains
- Cantaloupe, Banana and Pineapple Salad
- Cold Cucumber Salad Desert
- Green Bean Salad Forest
- Green Goddess Grape and Melon Pasture
- Raspberry Balsamic Watermelon Hills

Thanksgiving Dinner Board - pg 68
- Basil Roasted Carrot Hills
- Dressing Pastures
- Turkey Tenderloin Mountains

Vegetarian Southern Map - pg 45
- Pork Free Collard Green Forests
- Gluten Free Fried Okra Pastures (substitute almond milk for buttermilk)
- Vegetarian Red Beans and Rice Hills

Building Costs
- City Pasta - pg 84
- City Pot Pies - pg 86
- Cold Buckwheat Salad Road - pg 74
- Grilled Rosemary and Cherry Tomato Road - pg 72
- Grilled Asparagus and Bell Pepper Road - pg 73
- Lamb and Barley Development Card Stew - pg 91
- Lamb Kabobs Served on Pita - pg 92
- Lamb, Rice and Fig Pilaf - pg 93
- Moroccan Inspired City Lamb (without pita) - pg 85
- Panko Breaded Meatballs - pg 94
- Settlement Spinach Salad with Honeyed Apple Vinaigrette (without cheese) - pg 80
- Tomato and Cucumber Tree Lined Road (without cheese) - pg 75

Settlers of the Cold Salad (substitute sugar for honey) - pg 11
- Brown Lentil Mountains
- Cantaloupe, Banana and Pineapple Salad
- Cold Cucumber Salad Desert
- Green Bean Salad Forest
- Green Goddess Grape and Melon Pasture
- Raspberry Balsamic Watermelon Hills

Thanksgiving Dinner Board - pg 68
- Basil Roasted Carrot Hills
- Dressing Pastures

Vegetarian Southern Map - pg 45
- Pork Free Collard Green Forests
- Gluten Free Fried Okra Pastures (substitute almond milk for buttermilk)
- Vegetarian Red Beans and Rice Hills

Building Costs
- City Pasta - pg 84
- Cold Buckwheat Salad Road - pg 74
- Grilled Rosemary and Cherry Tomato Road - pg 72
- Grilled Asparagus and Bell Pepper Road - pg 73
- Settlement Spinach Salad with Honeyed Apple Vinaigrette (without cheese) - pg 80
- Tomato and Cucumber Tree Lined Road (without cheese) - pg 75

VEGETARIAN - 84 recipes

All American Meatloaf Map - pg 30
- Clove and Honey Pea Pastures
- Garlic Butter Asparagus Forest
- Sweet Corn Fields

Barbecue Board - pg 42
- Coleslaw Pasture
- Pesto Pasta Salad Forest
- Potato Salad Fields

Biscuit Bar - pg 18
- Buttermilk Hex Biscuits
- Herbed Hex Compound Butter
- Home Made Honey Butter

Breakfast Taco Map - pg 21
- Guacamole Pastures
- Salsafied Hills
- Sausage-ish Mountains

Deconstructed Paella Board - pg 60
- Entire Board

Deconstructed Salad Nicoise - pg 33
- Everything but the Tuna

Fish Fry Board - pg 35
- Broccoli Slaw Pastures
- Garlic and Herb Filled Pull-Apart Rolls
- Garlic and Lemon Red Skinned Potatoes Hills and Green Beans Forests
- Tartar Sauce Desert

Home Made Chips and Dips Map - pg 57
- Basil Spinach Dip Pastures
- Black Bean Dip Mountains
- Ranch Desert

Indian Inspired Map - pg 63
- Chana Masala Mountains
- Chapatis
- Cucumber Salad Pasture
- Curried Green Bean Forest
- Raita Desert
- Saffron Rice Fields
- Vegan Dal Hills

Mediterranean Map - pg 27
- Cucumber Salad Forest
- Tzaziki Desert
- Roasted Red Bell Pepper Hummus Hills

Pasta Board - pg 49
- Alfredo Desert
- Basil Marinara Hills
- Garlic Butter Fields
- Pesto Pastures

Quick Bread Board - pg 39
- Basil Pesto Garlic Forests
- Banana Bread Fields
- Hazelnut Crusted Chocolate Mountains
- Jalapeno Cornbread Pastures
- Maraschino Cherry Hills

Roasted Root Vegetable Board - pg 52
- Browned Butter Whole Wheat Yeast Rolls
- Herb Roasted Yellow Carrot Fields
- Herb Roasted Yellow Potato Pasture

1-UP MUSHROOM PIZZA ROLLS

When you need energy to make it through the Mushroom Kingdom on your way to rescue Princess Peach (again), level up your game with these One Up Mushroom Pizza Rolls.

1 can refrigerated biscuits

1 cup mushrooms, diced

1/2 cup onions, diced

2 tbsp butter

1 tbsp Italian Seasoning

20 slices pepperoni

5 slices mozzarella cheese

1/2 cup basil pesto

6 drops green food coloring

edible ball bearings

unch small circles
each slice of
Save both the
nd the circles.

Melt the butter in a large skillet.

Saute mushrooms and onions over a medium-high heat until the onions start to brown and the mushrooms lose some of their moisture. Add Italian seasoning and cook another minute.

Flatten a refrigerated biscuit. Put a slice of pepperoni in the middle. Add a tablespoon of the mushroom mix on top of the pepperoni.

See all that leftover mozzarella cheese? Add a couple scraps. Put another piece of pepperoni on top.

Pinch the biscuit dough closed around the top slice of pepperoni.

Put the stuffed biscuit in a mini-muffin tray, pinched side down. Bake at 375F for 14-18 minutes, or until the biscuits are golden brown.

While the biscuits bake, add your green food coloring to the basil pesto.

As soon as the biscuits come out of the oven, and before you remove them from the tray, use a pastry brush to paint the tops with basil pesto.

Add five cheese circles. Let the tray fully cool before removing.

Before serving, press two edible ball bearings into the base for the eyes.

WAIT! THAT'S PRIME REAL ESTATE!

These make great snacks for kart racing, intergalactic exploration, or smashing your brother in a brawl.

Made in the USA
Lexington, KY
10 January 2014